chef WAN

simply sedap

Chef Wan's favourite recipes

chef WAN

simply sedap

Chef Wan's favourite recipes

Marshall Cavendish Cuisine

The publisher wishes to thank Kitchen Culture Sdn Bhd for the use of their premises for the photos on cover and page 2; Syarikat Pemasaran Karyaneka Sdn Bhd, Malaysia; Langkawi Crystal, Malaysia; Wan Latifah Ramli and Florence Tan for the loan of their crockery and utensils.

All photographs by Jenhor Siow, except for photos on cover and page 2 by Pacino Wong of You Studio

Published by Marshall Cavendish Cuisine
An imprint of Marshall Cavendish International

Other Marshall Cavendish Offices:
Marshall Cavendish International. PO Box 65829 London EC1P 1NY, UK • Marshall Cavendish Corporation. 99 White Plains Road, Tarrytown NY 10591-9001, USA • Marshall Cavendish International (Thailand) Co Ltd. 253 Asoke, 12th Flr, Sukhumvit 21 Road, Klongtoey Nua, Wattana, Bangkok 10110, Thailand • Marshall Cavendish (Malaysia) Sdn Bhd, Times Subang, Lot 46, Subang Hi-Tech Industrial Park, Batu Tiga, 40000 Shah Alam, Selangor Darul Ehsan, Malaysia

Marshall Cavendish is a trademark of Times Publishing Limited

National Library Board Singapore Cataloguing in Publication Data

Wan, Chef, 1958-
Simply sedap / Chef Wan. – Singapore : Marshall Cavendish Cuisine, 2012, c2000.
p. cm.
Includes index.
ISBN : 978-981-4361-52-1

1. Cooking. I. Title.

TX714
641.5 -- dc22   OCN761358735

Printed in Singapore by KWF Printing Pte Ltd

simply sedap

sedap /sə ndaːp/, adj. appetising, delectable, delicious, full of flavour, lip-smacking good, mouthwatering, palatable, scrumptious; describes a state of culinary nirvana usually attained after partaking of a memorable meal.

CONTENTS

To my friend
Neil Monahan
who made me
what I am
Today

My continuing love of home cooking and all the joys inherent in it have inspired this book. I believe that cooking is one of life's great pleasures and that it can fit comfortably into the lifestyle of everyone, even the busiest person. The worlds of home cooking and active working life need not be mutually exclusive. The prevailing trend against cooking and eating at home, the dismissal of them as mere chores, strikes me as a sad symptom of a world that moves too fast. The rituals of cooking and eating together at home enrich our lives. They transform a house into a home, a stranger into a friend. They provide unique opportunities for communication and fulfilment, both for the home cook and for those who enjoy the food. I constantly feel the strength of these values in my personal life.

Ever since I can remember, I have dreamed of being a cook. At the age of five I used to play *masak-masak* (play cooking) with my sister and our neighbour's daughter, where I played the role of cook. At seven, I suggested that we steal some food from our mother's kitchen and cook up a storm in the backyard. I consistently ignored my parents' advice not to play with fire. By the age of nine, I was assisting my parents in our vegetable garden. We cleared new plots of land, cutting and burning the grass and raking the soil. Before we knew it, we had vegetables growing like weeds and I got busy selling vegetables every evening in our neighbourhood. It was a wonderful experience to see the fruits of our labour. And, of course, the fresh, home-grown vegetables tasted delicious.

PREFACE

Two or three days a week I went fishing with my father after work to a nearby *lombong* (quarry), so we were never short of things to eat. In a small part of the vegetable garden, we even started raising free-range chickens. Had it not been for the shortage of space, Chef Wan would have had an 'Old Macdonald's farm' complete with cows and goats back then!

After the day's work the nine of us sat at the dinner table eagerly awaiting the pleasure of eating. Food was heaven to me. Though I may not then have had the words to express it, nor the capacity to fully understand the meaning, I could sense the pride in my parents' eyes as they looked at us wolfing down everything that was laid in front of us. Back then, my mother and our neighbours always shared the extra food they had. The food was not fancy; it was just fresh and cooked with care and love. Today, such meals provide a welcome respite from the pressured and impersonal world that we live in.

Until today, every time I visit my mother I request her to make the nasi goreng (fried rice) that I grew up with—a simple dish with *ikan bilis* (anchovy), *belacan* (shrimp paste) and chilli. Never mind that I now have more elaborate nasi goreng recipes. Because hers is prepared with love and care, I have three helpings!

I always stress to parents that no matter how busy they are, they must prepare some special food for their children so that they will remember them for a long time. Never mind if initially it doesn't taste great. Practice makes perfect. As we say in Malay, "*Sentuhan tangan ibu itu amat penting. Di sinilah lahirnya kasih sayang di antara ibu dan anak* (A mother's touch is very important. From it comes the love between mother and child)."

It worries me to see the lack of family values these days. Most parents take the easy way out. We are slaves to the frozen and hygienically sealed food at the supermarket, to the fast-food giants. All they do is create a distance between food and diners. The high plastic counters, the disposable plates and forks, the emphasis on minimal contact between food and human hands to ensure 'cleanliness and hygiene' … all these things create an estrangement between the diners and those who prepare the food, to say nothing of the estrangement between the cooks and the food itself.

At the supermarket, when I see housewives piling their carts high with mass-produced artificial food, I feel like saying, "Please … take a second look at what you're buying! Is this really what you want to feed your family?" It's frustrating for me. Food should be experienced through all the senses, and I feel sorry for those who cannot see this. It is unfortunate for children who will never know the taste of real food. They will grow up believing that the mass-produced imitation, the phoney, is the real thing. As a result of the rush to prepare food and the rush to consume it, communication around the dinner table, and the sense of family and friendship that comes with it, are largely missing in today's society.

Cooking is a matter of trusting your own sensibilities. It is observing, tasting, touching, smelling and experiencing the ingredients for yourself and noticing what happens to them as they are cooked. Similarly, seasoning—with salt, pepper, chilli, vinegar, herbs, spices, sugar—is essentially a matter of personal taste. Be careful not to get caught up in comparing how something tastes with an imaginary arbitrary standard. Instead, simply observe how each seasoning affects the flavour of the dish and decide for yourself on the level of seasoning you like.

Remember, flexibility is an essential component of good cooking. You should never feel locked into a recipe or a menu unless it involves basic principles regarding procedure or technique, such as those involved in pastry making. When you are faced with the absence of a certain ingredient, don't panic. Formulate your own acceptable or inspired replacement, always with the harmony and balance of the dish in mind.

Cooking is a subjective experience, since we all cook differently. I may prefer a slightly saltier taste than you do, for instance. I have often tasted the same dish prepared by different cooks using the same recipe. The results were similar, but they were not identical. A word of advice: Learn to trust your own instincts rather than trying to please someone else.

A good cook need only have positive feelings about food in general; he need not be particularly enamoured by eating. I have known many cooks who, despite their years in the profession, have failed to discover gratification in their art. Remember, a cook who dislikes food is a bad cook. Period. Even an ambivalent cook is a bad cook.

This book is my private collection of recipes obtained over the last thirty years, since I first started cooking. Some have been created, some have been recreated, some have been stolen from friends, while others have been begged for. The things they all have in common are that they taste wonderful, they are based on fresh ingredients and they are prepared using a practical, common-sense approach.

I hope this book will enhance your pleasure in cooking, which can be fun and satisfying. I would like the recipes to be understood by someone who doesn't know how to cook at all: the absence of technical knowledge should not deter anyone from experiencing the pleasures of these dishes.

Let me share with you a comment made by one of my professors during my graduation in 1989: "There is a lot to think about and a lot to get done, but to be efficient does not mean to be hurried, and to be unhurried does not mean to sit in a lawn chair. Take the time to give each task its due—it comes out in the food, it shows a generosity of spirit. Call it rejoicing tenderness, graciousness or simple attention to detail—the quality of caring is an ingredient everyone can taste."

For the completion of this book, which seems to have been a nightmare for everyone, I wish to thank the following people:

my two beautiful children, Mohd Nadzri and Serina, who understand my life and career and never ask for more;

Jamilah Mohd Hassan and Christine Chong of Times Editions, for their infinite patience, their belief in me and all their wonderful work in making this book a reality;

Tuck Loong, for his food styling and his brilliant and diligent execution of the design work (How about a third book?);

Jen Seow, the best in Malaysia, for his creative photography.

Lastly, I would like to thank the journalists and all my ardent fans, old, young, big, small … for their kind support that has helped me get where I am today. *Terima kasih, terima kasih semua* (Thank you, thank you all).

WEIGHTS & MEASURES

Quantities in this book are given in Metric, Imperial and American (spoon and cup) measures. Standard spoon and cup measurements used are: 1 teaspoon = 5 ml, 1 tablespoon = 15 ml, 1 cup = 250 ml. All measures are level unless otherwise stated.

LIQUID AND VOLUME MEASURES

Metric	Imperial	American
5 ml	$^1/_6$ fl oz	1 teaspoon
10 ml	$^1/_3$ fl oz	1 dessertspoon
15 ml	$^1/_2$ fl oz	1 tablespoon
60 ml	2 fl oz	$^1/_4$ cup (4 tablespoons)
85 ml	$2^1/_2$ fl oz	$^1/_3$ cup
90 ml	3 fl oz	$^3/_8$ cup (6 tablespoons)
125 ml	4 fl oz	$^1/_2$ cup
180 ml	6 fl oz	$^3/_4$ cup
250 ml	8 fl oz	1 cup
300 ml	10 fl oz ($^1/_2$ pint)	$1^1/_4$ cups
375 ml	12 fl oz	$1^1/_2$ cups
435 ml	14 fl oz	$1^3/_4$ cups
500 ml	16 fl oz	2 cups
625 ml	20 fl oz (1 pint)	$2^1/_2$ cups
750 ml	24 fl oz ($1^1/_5$ pints)	3 cups
1 litre	32 fl oz ($1^3/_5$ pints)	4 cups
1.25 litres	40 fl oz (2 pints)	5 cups
1.5 litres	48 fl oz ($2^2/_5$ pints)	6 cups
2.5 litres	80 fl oz (4 pints)	10 cups

DRY MEASURES

Metric	Imperial
30 grams	1 ounce
45 grams	$1^1/_2$ ounces
55 grams	2 ounces
70 grams	$2^1/_2$ ounces
85 grams	3 ounces
100 grams	$3^1/_2$ ounces
110 grams	4 ounces
125 grams	$4^1/_2$ ounces
140 grams	5 ounces
280 grams	10 ounces
450 grams	16 ounces (1 pound)
500 grams	1 pound, $1^1/_2$ ounces
700 grams	$1^1/_2$ pounds
800 grams	$1^3/_4$ pounds
1 kilogram	2 pounds, 3 ounces
1.5 kilograms	3 pounds, $4^1/_2$ ounces
2 kilograms	4 pounds, 6 ounces

OVEN TEMPERATURE

	°C	°F	Gas Regulo
Very slow	120	250	1
Slow	150	300	2
Moderately slow	160	325	3
Moderate	180	350	4
Moderately hot	190/200	370/400	5/6
Hot	210/220	410/440	6/7
Very hot	230	450	8
Super hot	250/290	475/550	9/10

LENGTH

Metric	Imperial
0.5 cm	$^1/_4$ inch
1 cm	$^1/_2$ inch
1.5 cm	$^3/_4$ inch
2.5 cm	1 inch

SALADS

18

Som Tam
(Traditional Thai Papaya Salad)

Kerabu Udang dan
Mangga Muda
(Prawn [Shrimp] and Mango Salad)

Kerabu Ikan Kembung
(Chubb Mackerel Salad)

20

Lawar
(Balinese Vegetable and Chicken Salad)

Kerabu Daging Salai
Bersama Mangga
(Barbecued Beef and Mango Salad)

Larb Kai
(Chiengmai-Style Chicken Salad)

22

Meshoui Salad

Kerabu Sotong
(Cuttlefish Salad)

Hawaiian Chicken Salad

24

Kerabu Pucuk Paku dan
Udang Nyonya
(Nyonya Ferntop and Prawn [Shrimp] Salad)

Mediterranean Squid Salad

26

Nicoise Salad

Grilled Prawn (Shrimp) Salad
with Mango Vinaigrette

Umai Ikan
(Sarawak Raw Fish Salad)

SALADS

I must admit that, being an Asian, I did not grow up being a great fan of salads. Only in the last five years have I learned to appreciate them and realise how much I've been missing out on. Today, salads in their various incarnations play an important part in the urban Malaysian diet. If you take a walk to your nearest supermarket you're bound to see a variety of salad greens on the shelves.

A salad can be a whole meal, a starter, an accompaniment to the main course or even a refresher after it. Green salads should be dressed lightly just before serving—or even at the table. I love preparing a Caesar's salad at the table when guests are sitting down for dinner. (By the way, my friends say I make the best Caesar's salad in town!)

When making a leafy salad, the greens should be more or less bite sized, torn by hand rather than chopped so that they don't get discoloured. The leaves should look clean and fresh and should be properly chilled. Non-leafy vegetables, raw or cooked, can also be used in salads. If they are raw, they should be young and tender. Cooked vegetables should have a crisp texture and bright colour; they should not be overcooked.

In this chapter I've included some of my favourite recipes for composed salads. A composed salad is one in which the ingredients have been combined in advance and which can be served as it is.

In some of the other salads, the vegetables are combined in advance and the dressing is added just before serving. Dressings are an easy way of making foods more exciting and interesting, highlighting their intrinsic flavour. They can be flavoured in an almost infinite number of ways, using ingredients from around the world. They have to be prepared and used with care. A good dressing can make a salad, by adding a touch of originality, freshness and distinction, but a bad one can spoil it by being insipid or too heavy. A salad dressing can transform simple ingredients into a special treat, vegetables into an exotic dish. However good a dressing, do not add so much that the taste of the salad ingredients is drowned.

The two most widely used salad dressings are the simple French dressing (oil and vinegar) and mayonnaise. From both these dressings, you can devise many variations. For example, the character can be varied enormously by using different types of oil and vinegar; using fruit juices such as lemon, lime and orange; using different types of mustard; and, of course, adding flavouring ingredients such as herbs, spices, garlic and shallots. But dressings can also have flavours as diverse as Chinese, Indian, Thai, East meets West, Middle Eastern and Mediterranean. Try to make salad dressing about 30 minutes before it is to be used, to allow the flavours to develop.

Salads are not the only food that dressings can be used with. Dressings can also be served over or with grilled, baked or roasted meat, poultry, game, fish and vegetables.

The opportunity to choose from such a wide range of possibilities can make a green salad a wonderfully complex and colourful dish. Its composition depends on your taste and what is available. Today, a large assortment of vinegars, differing widely in flavour, strength and character, is available on the supermarket shelf. A soft, mild vinegar, such as champagne vinegar or white wine vinegar, goes well with tender, delicate lettuce. Greens that have a stronger leaf structure and taste can better support and are complemented by a strong vinegar, such as an aged red wine vinegar or a sherry vinegar, used with a heavier, fruitier olive oil. You need not be limited to a single vinegar per salad. You can combine vinegars, using one as a base and another for its particular sharpness, sweetness or flavour.

Oils can also be mixed together to good effect. For example, walnut and hazelnut oils can either be blended with olive oil or used alone. The correct proportion of oil to vinegar is commonly taken to be three parts oil to one part vinegar, and this can be used as a rough guide. In addition, there is your own palate to consider and what you find to be an acceptable level of acidity. This is why recipes for dressings in several cookbooks suggest a final taste to check the balance of flavours and seasoning before serving.

As for choice of vegetables, there is an abundant variety of greens to choose from in the supermarket. In addition to the normal *daun salad*—what the Malays call the leafy green lettuce—we also have iceberg, Boston and Romaine lettuce. Occasionally we get what I call the 'designer greens'—red oak leaf, green lollo, endive and butter crunch. However, we will not go into details here, since most of my recipes call for just simple green lettuce.

Kerabu are Asian-style salads, made using local ingredients. My late grandmother loved kerabu and sayur ulam. Made with blanched or raw vegetables, she had to have them with a small plate of sambal belacan to boost her appetite at dinner. In fact, she grew her own *ulam* (indigenous plants) in her backyard and ate them every day. Today, *ulam* and kerabu are no longer confined to the rickety dining tables of antiquated Malay *kampung* homes; they can be nibbled in the plushest of restaurants.

Ulam is actually a generic term for the whole gamut of indigenous edible plants that are eaten raw with sambal. These greens include a number of vegetables, herbaceous plants, wild plants and even fruit. The parts of the plants savoured most for their individual delicate (and sometimes not so delicate) flavours are the roots, stems, leaves and shoots. *Ulam* is the Malay equivalent of the ubiquitous Western green salad. Nasi ulam, as the name suggests, is a dish of rice mixed with many varieties of *ulam* and other herbs and spices.

And what about kerabu? The confusion starts here. More than one variety of *ulam* blended together and eaten raw is known as kerabu. Similarly, if this is mixed with rice, *santan* (coconut milk) and prawns, it is known as nasi kerabu, which is very popular on the east coast of Malaysia. As with many indigenous dishes, the names often differ from state to state. On the east coast, in the states of Kelantan and Terengganu, for example, nasi ulam is often synonymous with nasi kerabu.

When preparing different *ulam* for a kerabu dish, it is vital to balance the ingredients and flavour. On some leisurely Sundays I, like my grandmother, like to consume a variety of sayur ulam. I have them with anything hot and sour (*asam pedas*) or simply with grilled fish.

Ulam not only offers certain health benefits, it also provides (depending on the variety) a high amount of minerals, such as calcium, potassium and iron, and vitamins A and C. As in the case of most vegetables, *ulam* is very low in fat and protein, which adds to its appeal amongst the health conscious. Some *ulam* also have medicinal value. For example, traditional belief has it that *ulam raja* (*Cosmos caudatus*), *petai* (parkia) and *jering* (*Pithecellobium jiringa*) are good for diabetes patients; *daun pegaga* (Indian pennywort—*Centella asiatica*) is said to be good for flatulence; *pucuk betik* (young papaya leaf) is a remedy for high blood pressure; and *kacang botol* (four-angled bean) increases stamina.

Now I finally understand how my grandmother survived to be ninety-six. In fact, had it not been for the snake that bit her in the bushes, she would probably still be munching her *ulam*! Kerabu dishes bring back wonderful memories of my grandmother.

Ever since I came home to Malaysia after my graduation, I've been collecting delicious kerabu recipes from all over Asean. I hope you enjoy them as much as I do.

SOM TAM
(Traditional Thai Papaya Salad)

This is a traditional Thai salad, sold as a snack everywhere in Thailand and often served as a side dish with barbecued chicken, meat or seafood. It is so popular that it is even sold by the roadside, especially in Bangkok. It is prepared in a large mortar, but the method of preparation differs from one region to another. The papaya used ranges from raw green to slightly ripe, but it is always firm in texture to ensure a crunchy salad. Sometimes a small live mud crab is added. While kicking away, it is pounded to pieces together with the salad!

Ingredients

3 cloves garlic, peeled

30 grams/1 ounce/$\frac{1}{4}$ cup dried prawns (shrimps), soaked in water and drained

4–6 bird's eye chillies

85 grams/3 ounces/$\frac{1}{2}$ cup peanuts, roasted

3 tablespoons grated palm sugar or brown sugar

2 tomatoes, cut into wedges

1 tablespoon tamarind juice, extracted from 1 teaspoon tamarind pulp and 1 tablespoon water

2–3 tablespoons nam pla

juice of 1–2 limes

350–425 grams/12–15 ounces/4–5 cups peeled, shredded green papaya

long beans

Method

1. Pound the garlic, dried prawns (shrimps), chillies, peanuts and palm sugar or brown sugar until coarsely ground. Add the tomatoes and continue pounding to make the mixture smooth.

2. Add the tamarind juice, *nam pla* and lime juice. Stir and transfer to a salad bowl.

3. Add the papaya and mix well. Serve with raw long beans.

KERABU UDANG DAN MANGGA MUDA
(Prawn [Shrimp] and Mango Salad)

This kerabu originates from the famous som tam (papaya salad) of Thailand. Besides freshwater prawns (shrimps), the Thais also like to use freshwater catfish (*Clarias batrachus*). This kerabu goes well on top of deep-fried catfish. If catfish is not available, grouper or sea bass can be used.

Ingredients

500 grams/1 pound, 1$\frac{1}{2}$ ounces freshwater prawns (shrimps), blanched and drained

2 unripe mangoes, peeled and finely sliced

2 kaffir lime leaves, finely sliced

15 grams/$\frac{1}{2}$ ounce/$\frac{1}{4}$ cup chopped coriander leaves (cilantro)

2 tablespoons chopped mint leaves

60 ml/2 fl oz/$\frac{1}{4}$ cup nam pla

juice of 2 limes

salt

sugar

200 grams/7 ounces/4$\frac{1}{2}$ cups glass noodles, blanched and drained

55 grams/2 ounces/$\frac{1}{2}$ cup crisp-fried shallots

salad greens

85 grams/3 ounces/$\frac{1}{2}$ cup peanuts, roasted and pounded

Finely Pounded Paste

3 red chillies

3 bird's eye chillies

45 grams/1$\frac{1}{2}$ ounces/$\frac{3}{8}$ cup dried prawns (shrimps), soaked in water and drained

3 cloves garlic, peeled

3 tablespoons grated palm sugar or brown sugar

2 tomatoes, quartered

Method

1. Mix all the ingredients except peanuts and salad greens with the finely pounded paste.

2. Line a serving dish with salad greens, place the kerabu on top and sprinkle with peanuts. Serve immediately.

Note: It is best to mix the kerabu just before serving, to prevent it from becoming soggy and to keep the mango crunchy.

KERABU IKAN KEMBUNG
(Chubb Mackerel Salad)

Ingredients

6 chubb mackerel, cleaned and deep-fried until crisp

6 shallots, peeled and finely sliced

2 red chillies, finely chopped

4 bird's eye chillies, sliced

85 grams/3 ounces/$\frac{1}{2}$ cup peanuts, roasted and pounded

2 unripe mangoes, peeled and finely sliced

juice of 2–3 limes

1 torch ginger bud, sliced

handful of mint leaves, finely chopped

3 tablespoons nam pla

2 tomatoes, finely diced

1 teaspoon sugar

1 stalk lemon grass, finely sliced

Method

Bone and shred the fish and toss with the remaining ingredients until well mixed. Serve immediately.

Opposite: Kerabu Udang dan Mangga Muda (Prawn [Shrimp] and Mango Salad).

LAWAR
(Balinese Vegetable and Chicken Salad)

Ingredients

3 tablespoons cooking oil

2 *salam* leaves

250 ml/8 fl oz/1 cup coconut milk,
extracted from $^1/_2$ grated coconut and
250 ml/8 fl oz/1 cup water

300 grams/10$^1/_2$ ounces chicken breast,
finely diced

salt

sugar

200 grams/7 ounces long beans,
cut into 0.5-cm/$^1/_4$-inch lengths

300 grams/10$^1/_2$ ounces young jackfruit,
peeled, blanched and cut into bite-
sized pieces

45 grams/1$^1/_2$ ounces/$^1/_2$ cup roasted
grated or desiccated coconut

30 grams/1 ounce/$^1/_4$ cup crisp-fried
shallots

6 bird's eye chillies, whole or finely sliced

lime juice

Finely Ground Paste

5 red chillies

$^1/_2$ teaspoon black peppercorns

3 candlenuts

6 shallots, peeled

4 cloves garlic, peeled

1 cm/$^1/_2$ inch galangal, peeled

1 cm/$^1/_2$ inch fresh turmeric, peeled

1 stalk lemon grass, finely sliced

2 tablespoons grated palm sugar
or brown sugar

Method

1. Heat the oil and fry the finely ground
   paste until fragrant. Add the *salam*
   leaves, coconut milk and chicken.
   Cook until slightly thickened and
   season with salt and sugar. Remove
   from heat and cool.

2. Put the long beans and jackfruit in a
   bowl. Add the chicken, coconut, crisp-
   fried shallots and chillies, and toss.
   Season with lime juice.

Note: Finely shredded turmeric leaves and roasted
grated coconut may be sprinkled on top of this
salad before serving.

KERABU DAGING SALAI BERSAMA MANGGA
(Barbecued Beef and Mango Salad)

Ingredients

500 grams/1 pound, 1$^1/_2$ ounces beef
loin, finely sliced

2 ripe mangoes, peeled and sliced

2 tomatoes, cut into wedges

2 stalks lemon grass, finely sliced

55 grams/2 ounces/1 cup chopped
mint leaves

4 spring onions (scallions),
finely chopped

salad greens

Marinade (blended)

1 tablespoon nam pla

2 tablespoons sweet soy sauce

2 tablespoons cooking oil

1 tablespoon caster
(super fine) sugar

Dressing (blended)

2 tablespoons *nam pla*

juice of 2 limes

3 tablespoons grated palm sugar or
brown sugar

3 cloves garlic, peeled and finely chopped

2 tablespoons roasted sesame seeds

Method

1. Mix the beef with the marinade and
   set aside for about 10 minutes.

2. Roast over glowing charcoal for
   30 seconds on each side.

3. Into a bowl containing the dressing,
   add the barbecued beef, mangoes,
   tomatoes, lemon grass, mint leaves
   and spring onions (scallions). Mix well
   and place on a serving dish lined with
   salad greens. Serve immediately.

LARB KAI
(Chiengmai-Style Chicken Salad)

This salad is a favourite with farmers in
northern Thailand.

Ingredients

250 grams/9 ounces chicken breast,
finely chopped

10 shallots, peeled and finely sliced

2 spring onions (scallions), finely sliced

juice of $^1/_4$ lime

$^1/_2$ teaspoon powdered chilli

55 grams/2 ounces/$^1/_4$ cup rice, roasted
until brown and finely pounded

handful of coriander leaves (cilantro),
finely chopped

2–3 tablespoons *nam pla*

handful of mint leaves, finely chopped

salad greens

Method

1. Heat a wok (without oil) and cook the
   chicken until dry. Remove to a bowl.

2. Add all the other ingredients except
   salad greens and toss. Transfer to a
   serving dish lined with salad greens.

Note: The chicken can be substituted with minced
(ground) beef or pork. Sometimes the roasted rice
is substituted with roasted glutinous rice.

Opposite: Lawar (Balinese Vegetable and Chicken Salad).

MESHOUI SALAD

In 1992 I started my first TV programme, *Food of the World*, on a Malaysian TV station. The six-month series covered the cuisine and cultural background of twenty-six countries. Among my guests was the Moroccan ambassador's wife, Laila Sairi. I prepared Lamb Kefta with Chicken Couscous, while Laila made this wonderful salad. It was not only aromatic, due to the grilled capsicum (bell pepper), but also incredibly delicious and refreshing.

Ingredients

    2 green capsicums (bell peppers)
    2 red capsicums (bell peppers)
    6 large ripe tomatoes, seeded and diced
    1 large cucumber, seeded and finely diced
    2 onions, peeled and finely chopped
    55 grams/2 ounces/$^1/_2$ cup chopped
        parsley
    55 grams/2 ounces/$^1/_2$ cup chopped
        spring onions (scallions)
    2 eggs, hard-boiled, shelled and chopped
    Salad Dressing*

Method

1. Grill the green and red capsicums (bell peppers) over the stove until thoroughly black. Put into a plastic bag and set aside to 'sweat' for 20 minutes.

2. Remove the capsicums (bell peppers) from the bag and peel off the skin. Do not use any water when peeling them, to retain the char-grilled aroma.

3. Cut each capsicum (bell pepper) in two, remove the seeds and dice.

4. Place the capsicums (bell peppers) in a salad bowl together with the tomatoes, cucumber, onions, parsley, spring onions (scallions) and eggs.

5. Just before serving, toss in the dressing and mix well.

*SALAD DRESSING

Ingredients

    juice of 1 large lemon
    $^1/_2$ teaspoon or slightly more salt
    freshly cracked black pepper
    pinch of sugar
    60 ml/2 fl oz/$^1/_4$ cup extra virgin olive oil

Method

1. In a bowl, mix together the lemon juice, salt, pepper and sugar.

2. Gradually whisk in the oil, so that the dressing emulsifies.

KERABU SOTONG
(Cuttlefish Salad)

Ingredients

    500 grams/1 pound, 1$^1/_2$ ounces
        cuttlefish, cut into bite-sized pieces,
        boiled and chilled
    1 unripe mango, peeled and shredded
    30 grams/1 ounce/$^1/_4$ cup dried prawns
        (shrimps), fried
    1 red onion, peeled and finely sliced
    2 stalks lemon grass, finely sliced
    2 kaffir lime leaves, sliced
    handful of mint leaves, chopped

Dressing (blended)

    2 tablespoons *nam pla*
    2 tablespoons sugar
    3 cloves garlic, peeled and finely chopped
    2 tablespoons roasted sesame seeds
    juice of 2 limes
    2 tablespoons light soy sauce

Method

1. Put all the salad ingredients in a bowl.

2. Add in the dressing, toss and serve.

HAWAIIAN CHICKEN SALAD

Ingredients

    3 chicken breasts, boiled, cooled and diced
    170 grams/6 ounces/1 cup peeled, diced
        ripe papaya
    140 grams/5 ounces/1 cup diced
        pineapple
    1 avocado, stoned, peeled and diced
    2 tomatoes, diced
    2 tablespoons dark raisins
    1 spring onion (scallion), chopped
    1 celery stalk, diced
    $^1/_2$ ripe mango, peeled and diced
    2 tablespoons finely chopped coriander
        leaves (cilantro)

Dressing (blended)

    125 ml/4 fl oz/$^1/_2$ cup mayonnaise
    125 ml/4 fl oz/$^1/_2$ cup sour cream
    60 ml/2 fl oz/$^1/_4$ cup bottled mango
        chutney
    $^1/_2$ teaspoon powdered ginger
    1 teaspoon chicken or meat curry powder
    lime juice
    salt
    sugar

Method

1. Put all the ingredients except coriander leaves (cilantro) into a bowl containing salad dressing and mix well.

2. Garnish with coriander leaves (cilantro). Serve immediately.

Note: It is best to mix this salad just before serving, to avoid the salad juices settling at the bottom. This salad tastes best chilled.

Opposite: Hawaiian Chicken Salad.

KERABU PUCUK PAKU DAN UDANG NYONYA
(Nyonya Ferntop and Prawn [Shrimp] Salad)

This recipe belongs to my maternal grandmother, who is a third-generation Peranakan Nyonya. When I was young I often asked her to make this kerabu. While watching her prepare it, I insisted that I pounded the chillies. My grandmother had a huge *batu lesung* (granite mortar and pestle), which I was always crazy about. This year, after celebrating her ninetieth birthday, she finally decided to hand over the *batu lesung* to me.

Ingredients

- 200 grams/7 ounces *pucuk paku* (ferntops), cut and blanched
- 500 grams/1 pound, 1½ ounces large prawns (shrimps), blanched, shelled, deveined and halved
- 10 shallots, peeled and finely sliced
- 1 torch ginger bud, finely sliced
- 3 kaffir lime leaves, finely sliced
- juice of 4 kalamansi
- 125 ml/4 fl oz/½ cup coconut milk, extracted from ½ grated coconut and 125 ml/4 fl oz/½ cup water
- 110 grams/4 ounces/1 cup grated coconut, roasted
- 85 grams/3 ounces/½ cup roasted peanuts, coarsely pounded
- 1 tablespoon grated palm sugar or brown sugar
- salt

Coarsely Pounded Paste

- 5 red chillies
- 30 grams/1 ounce/¼ cup dried prawns (shrimps), soaked in water and drained
- 2 teaspoons shrimp paste

Method

Combine all the salad ingredients with the coarsely pounded paste and mix well. Serve immediately.

MEDITERRANEAN SQUID SALAD

Ingredients

- 500 grams/1 pound, 1½ ounces squid, blanched, drained and cut into rings
- 3 anchovy fillets, finely chopped
- 30 grams/1 ounce/¼ cup diced celery
- 2 tomatoes, quartered
- 10 green olives, pitted
- 10 black olives, pitted
- ½ green capsicum (bell pepper), sliced
- 1 lemon, sliced
- ¼ portion Oregano Dressing*
- ¼ portion Italian-Style Tomato Sauce**
- salad greens
- mint leaves, chopped
- fresh parsley, chopped

Method

1. Put the squid, anchovy, celery, tomatoes, olives, capsicum (bell pepper) and lemon in a bowl. Add Oregano Dressing and Italian-Style Tomato Sauce, and toss well.
2. Transfer to a serving dish lined with salad greens. Garnish with mint and parsley.

*OREGANO DRESSING

Ingredients

- 375 ml/12 fl oz/1½ cups cooking oil
- 125 ml/4 fl oz/½ cup olive oil
- 250 ml/8 fl oz/1 cup vegetable oil
- 125 ml/4 fl oz/½ cup mixture of redusive vinegar and orange juice
- 2 cloves garlic, peeled and finely chopped
- 1 tablespoon chopped fresh oregano

Method

Mix all the ingredients and blend well.

**ITALIAN-STYLE TOMATO SAUCE

Ingredients

- 60 ml/2 fl oz/¼ cup olive oil
- ½ onion, peeled and diced
- 3 cloves garlic, peeled and chopped
- 1 fresh bay leaf
- ½ teaspoon chopped (Western) basil leaves
- ½ teaspoon chopped fresh oregano
- ½ teaspoon chopped fresh thyme
- 1 can (411 grams/14½ ounces) Italian plum tomatoes, mashed
- ½ teaspoon cayenne pepper
- 1 teaspoon tomato purée (tomato paste)
- 250 ml/8 fl oz/1 cup water
- salt
- freshly cracked black pepper
- sugar
- 2 tablespoons chopped parsley

Method

1. Heat the oil and sauté the onion, garlic and herbs until soft.
2. Add the tomatoes, cayenne pepper, tomato purée (tomato paste) and water. Cook until the gravy thickens. Add salt, black pepper, sugar and parsley.

Note: The leftover Tomato Sauce and Oregano Dressing can be kept in an airtight container in the refrigerator. The Tomato Sauce can be used as a pasta sauce, and the Oregano Dressing can be used in a salad.

NICOISE SALAD

This salad, which originated in southern France, is sometimes used as a sandwich filling with French bread.

Ingredients

300 grams/10$\frac{1}{2}$ ounces long beans, cut, blanched in salted boiling water and drained

6 large tomatoes, quartered

$\frac{1}{2}$ green capsicum (bell pepper), sliced

$\frac{1}{2}$ red capsicum (bell pepper), sliced

1 medium cucumber, sliced

3 medium potatoes, boiled, peeled and cut into wedges

10 black olives, pitted

2 eggs, hard-boiled, shelled and halved

1 can (185 grams/6$\frac{1}{2}$ ounces) tuna, drained

3 anchovy fillets

salad greens

Salad Dressing*

fresh parsley, chopped (optional)

Method

1. Arrange the vegetables, olives, eggs, tuna and anchovy on a serving dish lined with salad greens.

2. Just before serving, pour dressing over the salad. Garnish with parsley (optional).

*SALAD DRESSING

Ingredients

1 clove garlic, peeled and chopped

1 teaspoon Dijon mustard

2 teaspoons chopped (Western) basil leaves

85 ml/2$\frac{1}{2}$ fl oz/$\frac{1}{3}$ cup redusive vinegar

salt

freshly cracked black pepper

250 ml/8 fl oz/1 cup extra virgin olive oil

Method

1. Combine the garlic, mustard and basil leaves. Add the vinegar, salt and pepper.

2. Gradually whisk in the oil, so that the dressing emulsifies.

GRILLED PRAWN (SHRIMP) SALAD WITH MANGO VINAIGRETTE

Ingredients

500 grams/1 pound, 1$\frac{1}{2}$ ounces large prawns (shrimps), shelled and deveined

1 head lettuce, torn into large pieces

1 cucumber, seeded and finely sliced

1 ripe mango, peeled and diced

3 tomatoes, seeded and finely sliced

Marinade (blended)

2 tablespoons chopped parsley

2 tablespoons honey

1 teaspoon Dijon mustard

1 tablespoon lemon juice

Mango Vinaigrette (blended)

4 shallots, peeled and finely chopped

$\frac{1}{2}$ teaspoon Dijon mustard

60 ml/2 fl oz/$\frac{1}{4}$ cup balsamic vinegar

60 ml/2 fl oz/$\frac{1}{4}$ cup cider vinegar

250 ml/8 fl oz/1 cup corn oil

2 ripe mangoes, peeled and diced

salt

freshly cracked black pepper

sugar

2 tablespoons chopped coriander leaves (cilantro)

Method

1. Mix the prawns (shrimps) with the marinade and set aside for 10 minutes. Grill them over glowing charcoal for 30 seconds on each side.

2. Arrange a dish with lettuce, cucumber, mango and tomatoes. Top with the prawns (shrimps). Drizzle half the mango vinaigrette over the salad and serve the rest in a sauceboat.

UMAI IKAN
(Sarawak Raw Fish Salad)

Ingredients

500 grams/1 pound, 1$\frac{1}{2}$ ounces freshwater fish, sliced

juice of 10 *kalamansi*

juice of 2 limes

3 red chillies, finely sliced

2 cm/1 inch ginger, peeled and finely sliced

7 shallots, peeled and sliced

salt

freshly cracked black pepper

1 sprig coriander leaves (cilantro), chopped

Method

1. Marinate the fish in *kalamansi* juice and lime juice until it turns white. Add the chillies, ginger and shallots. Season with salt and pepper. Set aside for at least 1 hour, preferably in the refrigerator.

2. Just before serving, garnish with coriander leaves (cilantro).

Note: For chilli lovers, you may add finely sliced bird's eye chillies.

SOUP

SOUP

Soup, soup, soup . . .
I love soup. In fact,
I had a bowl of
chicken soup just before
starting on this write-up.
To make it a complete and
balanced meal, I threw in
some vegetables—carrot, onion,
celery, potato—and a handful of
macaroni. With chicken as my source
of protein, macaroni for carbohydrates
and plenty of vegetables for fibre, what
could go wrong?

The best part is, soup takes only minutes
to prepare. Over my years of living alone, I have
found soup to be hearty as well as comforting.
Whether I am distressed, sick or simply in a hurry,
it plays an important role in my diet.

Gone are the days when I sat down before a big
plate of rice surrounded by four or five accompaniments.
Now I watch my waistline. It is most important that food be
nutritious and well balanced. I tell everyone that what matters
most is not the quantity of food that we eat but its quality. At
its very best, food is meant to gratify and soothe. Soup never fails
to satisfy. I am totally captivated by the seemingly simple charms of
soup, by both the ritual of making it and the ultimate reward of eating it.

I started making different kinds of soup when I was living in Vancouver
in 1990. I remember when I first arrived, it rained non-stop for almost
twenty-six days (*banjir-lo*! [It was flooded!]) until the first snow fell just before
Christmas. It was wet, cold and miserable, and all I could think of having when
I got home was a large bowl of soup.

The first few days I made plenty of chicken stock, with a lot of chicken carcass
and vegetables. Too often soup is made with tired old ingredients that can't be used
any other way, sort of refrigerator remnants. No wonder the result is terrible. I believe
that if something is not good enough to cook for its own sake, it is not good enough to put

into soup. It should go into the trash. Another reason why soup can be disappointing is that it is made with poor stock. Always remember the two essential ingredients for making wonderful soup: good stock and enough flavourful raw materials. Intensity is the key. If the soup is carrot, use plenty of carrot. If it is prawn (shrimp) bisque, use plenty of prawn (shrimp). You can't skimp on ingredients if you want to produce deeply flavourful soup.

Where were we? Oh yes, we talked about my soup orgy in the kitchen. So after making plenty of stock, I prepared four or five types of soup—ranging from a simple vegetable soup to a cream of mushroom as well as a bean soup. I survived on soup the whole week. What meals they were! Accompanied by good bread, soup can be satisfying indeed. The best part is, the following week I found I had lost 2 kilograms/4 pounds, 6 ounces, mostly from my waistline!

Making soup is easy, and most soups can be made ahead of time and reheated. And when you become an avid soup maker like me, just think of your waistline in the next two weeks!

Over the years I've created dozens of soup recipes. I even had a grand soup party one cold winter night in San Francisco. I invited fifty guests and served ten kinds of soup with ten varieties of bread. Everyone enjoyed it and took home leftovers.

A pressure cooker is the equipment of choice for soup making. Pressure cookers have been vastly improved over the years and are now safe, quiet and odourless. They cook soup in a fraction of the time taken by an ordinary soup pot, and they produce the most wonderful and well developed flavours. For example, my Oxtail Soup, which normally takes $1^1/_2$–2 hours to simmer over the stove, takes only 25 minutes in a pressure cooker. These days, when you cannot afford to waste any time and energy, the pressure cooker does take the pressure off!

Soups all over the world take many forms. Some are based on broth, e.g., consommé. Others are puréed and thickened with vegetables or a starch, such as rice and beans. Bisques usually have shellfish as their main ingredient.

Always remember, when you serve soup as a first course accompanied by a crusty roll or bread, just ladle a small portion. No matter how good it tastes, resist the temptation to serve more. It's only meant to tease the palate in anticipation of the second course. So don't ruin your dinner party by overfeeding your guests.

A word of advice: Moderate seasoning is the key to enhancing the flavours in the final dish. Add salt last, since the reduction of the stock concentrates it, sometimes making it sufficiently salty.

I could go on and on about soup, but we don't have the space for that. I hope you'll derive as much pleasure from making these soups as I have over the years. For a start, try out my Oxtail Soup. You'll love it … can you imagine all those cows roaming the countryside with no tails?

CORN CRAB SOUP

Ingredients

55 grams/2 ounces/¼ cup butter

1 onion, peeled and finely chopped

10 button mushrooms, finely sliced

1 litre/1³/₅ pints/4 cups chicken stock

250 ml/8 fl oz/1 cup fresh milk

1 can (425 grams/15 ounces) cream-style corn

3 crabs, steamed; reserve the meat

6 sprigs chive, finely chopped

2 tablespoons cornflour (cornstarch), mixed with 1 tablespoon water

salt

freshly cracked black pepper

spring onion (scallion), chopped

Method

1. Heat the butter in a soup pot and sauté the onion and mushrooms until soft.

2. Add the chicken stock and stir in the milk and corn. Boil for 10 minutes.

3. Add the crabmeat, chives and cornflour (cornstarch) mixture. Stir and season with salt and pepper.

4. Just before serving, garnish with spring onion (scallion).

MINESTRONE SOUP

Ingredients

90 ml/3 fl oz/³/₈ cup olive oil

3 onions, peeled and chopped

3 cloves garlic, peeled and finely chopped

4 tomatoes, chopped

¹/₂ teaspoon chopped fresh oregano

¹/₂ teaspoon chopped fresh thyme

¹/₂ teaspoon chopped (Western) basil leaves

410 grams/14 ounces/2 cups diced zucchini

200 grams/7 ounces/1 cup peeled, diced carrot

1 red capsicum (bell pepper), diced

2 potatoes, peeled and diced

100 grams/3¹/₂ ounces/¹/₂ cup button mushrooms, chopped

55 grams/2 ounces/¹/₄ cup drained canned kidney beans

1.5 litres/2²/₅ pints/6 cups chicken stock

2 tablespoons tomato purée (tomato paste)

2 tablespoons chopped parsley + extra for garnishing

1 fresh bay leaf

45 grams/1¹/₂ ounces/¹/₂ cup macaroni

salt

freshly cracked black pepper

grated Parmesan cheese

Method

1. Heat the oil in a soup pot and sauté the onions and garlic until fragrant. Add the tomatoes, oregano, thyme and basil.

2. Cook until almost dry. Add the vegetables, kidney beans, chicken stock, tomato purée (tomato paste), parsley, bay leaf and macaroni. Bring to a boil and simmer for 30–45 minutes.

3. Season with salt and pepper.

4. Just before serving, sprinkle with parsley and cheese.

MEATBALL SOUP

Ingredients

3 tablespoons olive oil

1 onion, peeled and finely chopped

3 cloves garlic, peeled and finely chopped

1 celery stalk, diced

1 carrot, peeled and diced

1.5 litres/2²/₅ pints/6 cups chicken stock

1 teaspoon chopped fresh thyme

1 tablespoon chopped parsley

1 fresh bay leaf

1 tablespoon chopped (Western) basil leaves

2 medium potatoes, peeled and diced

1 can (411 grams/14¹/₂ ounces) Italian plum tomatoes, mashed

15 Meatballs*

200 grams/7 ounces white cabbage, cut into large pieces

salt

freshly cracked black pepper

Method

1. Heat the oil in a soup pot and sauté the onion and garlic until fragrant.

2. Add the celery and carrot and cook for a few minutes before adding the chicken stock, thyme, parsley, bay leaf, basil, potatoes and tomatoes. Simmer for 10 minutes. While the soup is simmering, add the meatballs.

3. Add the cabbage and cook until the vegetables are tender. Season with salt and pepper.

*MEATBALLS

Ingredients

300 grams/10¹/₂ ounces minced (ground) beef

2 slices white bread, soaked in 3 tablespoons milk and mashed

¹/₂ onion, peeled and chopped

salt

freshly cracked black pepper

Method

1. Thoroughly mix all the ingredients and divide into 15 portions.

2. Shape each portion into a small ball.

Opposite: Minestrone Soup.

SOUP DE POISSON
(South of France Seafood Soup)

Although this soup has a French name, it is similar to the Italian Californian soup called *cioppino*. The secret in preparing this soup is to use good fish stock, fresh seafood and high-quality saffron.

Ingredients

60 ml/2 fl oz/$^1/_4$ cup olive oil
1 onion, peeled and finely chopped
3 cloves garlic, peeled and finely chopped
1 teaspoon chopped fresh thyme
1 teaspoon chopped (Western) basil leaves
1 fresh bay leaf
2 tablespoons finely chopped parsley
1 celery stalk, finely sliced
1 leek, finely chopped
1 can (411 grams/14$^1/_2$ ounces) Italian plum tomatoes, mashed
1 tablespoon tomato purée (tomato paste)
1 teaspoon saffron strands
1 litre/1$^3/_5$ pints/4 cups fish stock
125 ml/4 fl oz/$^1/_2$ cup white wine (optional)
2 crabs, halved
200 grams/7 ounces each: mussels, prawns (shrimps), fish fillet and squid
salt
freshly cracked black pepper

Method

1. Heat the oil in a soup pot and sauté the onion, garlic, thyme, basil, bay leaf, parsley, celery and leek until soft.
2. Add the tomatoes, tomato purée (tomato paste), saffron, fish stock and wine (optional). Simmer for 15 minutes.
3. Add the crabs, mussels, prawns (shrimps), fish fillet and squid. Season with salt and pepper and simmer for another 5 minutes. Serve hot with French loaf.

PALEMBANG FISH BALL SOUP

Ingredients

3 tablespoons cooking oil
4 cloves garlic, peeled and finely chopped
100 grams/3$^1/_2$ ounces prawns (shrimps), shelled and deveined
1 litre/1$^3/_5$ pints/4 cups water
100 grams/3$^1/_2$ ounces yam beans, peeled and cut into strips
30 grams/1 ounce/$^1/_2$ cup cloud ears, soaked in water and drained
45 grams/1$^1/_2$ ounces dried lily flowers
Fish Balls*
45 grams/1$^1/_2$ ounces/1 cup glass noodles
salt
freshly cracked black pepper
coriander leaves (cilantro), chopped
crisp-fried shallots

Method

1. Heat the oil in a soup pot and sauté the garlic and prawns (shrimps) until the prawns (shrimps) turn pink.
2. Add the water, yam beans, cloud ears and dried lily flowers. Boil for 5 minutes and add the fish balls. Boil for another 10 minutes and add the glass noodles. Season with salt and pepper.
3. Just before serving, garnish with coriander leaves (cilantro) and crisp-fried shallots.

*FISH BALLS

Ingredients

300 grams/10$^1/_2$ ounces mackerel fillet
2 teaspoons cornflour (cornstarch)
salt
freshly cracked black pepper
1 spring onion (scallion), finely chopped

Method

1. Pound the fish into a paste and mix thoroughly with all the other ingredients.
2. With wet hands, shape the mixture into small balls.

PRAWN (SHRIMP) SOUP

Ingredients

60 ml/2 fl oz/$^1/_4$ cup cooking oil
6 shallots, peeled and finely chopped
1 cm/$^1/_2$ inch young ginger, peeled and finely chopped
6 cloves garlic, peeled and finely chopped
3 tablespoons mixed ground soup spices
1.25 litres/2 pints/5 cups prawn (shrimp) stock
salt
freshly cracked black pepper
3 stalks lemon grass, bruised
30 grams/1 ounce/$^3/_8$ cup glass noodles
500 grams/1 pound, 1$^1/_2$ ounces medium prawns (shrimps), shelled and deveined

Method

1. Heat the oil in a soup pot and sauté the shallots, ginger and garlic until golden brown.
2. Add the soup spices and prawn (shrimp) stock and boil for 1 minute.
3. Season with salt and pepper and then add the lemon grass, glass noodles and prawns (shrimps). Simmer until the prawns (shrimps) are cooked.

Opposite: Soup de Poisson (South of France Seafood Soup).

CHEF WAN'S OXTAIL SOUP

Ingredients

125 ml/4 fl oz/$\frac{1}{2}$ cup vegetable oil

500 grams/1 pound, 1$\frac{1}{2}$ ounces oxtail, cleaned and cut into bite-sized pieces

2 tablespoons powdered coriander

1 tablespoon powdered cumin

1 tablespoon powdered fennel

1$\frac{1}{2}$ tablespoons tomato purée (tomato paste)

1.5 litres/2$\frac{2}{5}$ pints/6 cups water

1 carrot, peeled and diced

1 potato, peeled and diced

2 celery stalks, diced

salt

freshly cracked black pepper

coriander leaves (cilantro), chopped

crisp-fried shallots

Whole Spices

4 cardamoms

1 cm/$\frac{1}{2}$ inch cinnamon stick

6 cloves

2 star anise

Finely Ground Paste

10 shallots, peeled

4 cloves garlic, peeled

2 stalks lemon grass, finely sliced

1 cm/$\frac{1}{2}$ inch ginger, peeled

Method

1. Heat the oil in a soup pot and sear the oxtail until it browns slightly. Drain and set aside.

2. In the same oil, sauté the whole spices and finely ground paste until fragrant.

3. Add the coriander, cumin and fennel and sauté over low heat for 3–4 minutes until fragrant. Add the tomato purée (tomato paste).

4. Add the oxtail and water and bring to a simmer.

5. Add the carrot, potato and celery. Simmer over medium heat for 1 hour 45 minutes until the oxtail is tender. Season with salt and pepper.

6. Just before serving, garnish with coriander leaves (cilantro) and crisp-fried shallots.

Note: To save time, you can cook this soup in 25 minutes using a pressure cooker. You'll have to reduce the water to 1 litre/1$\frac{3}{5}$ pints/4 cups.

HARIRA
(Moroccan Lamb and Chickpea Soup)

This is a soup made especially during Ramadhan in Morocco. Old, traditional Mediterranean soups such as this one are rich and substantial, really more like stew than soup. Filled with vegetables, grains, leftover meat, they often constitute a main meal. Harira, sold in the open bazaars of Morocco, is often had at breakfast.

Ingredients

250 grams/9 ounces lamb, diced

3 litres/4$\frac{4}{5}$ pints/12 cups water

250 grams/9 ounces chickpeas, soaked in water overnight and drained

2 onions, peeled and diced

500 grams/1 pound, 1$\frac{1}{2}$ ounces tomatoes, chopped

3 sprigs coriander leaves (cilantro), chopped

$\frac{1}{2}$ teaspoon powdered turmeric

2.5 cm/1 inch ginger, peeled and finely chopped

freshly cracked black pepper

125 grams/4$\frac{1}{2}$ ounces rice vermicelli

2 tablespoons tomato purée (tomato paste)

salt

$\frac{1}{2}$ sprig parsley, chopped

Method

1. Boil the lamb in water for a few minutes. Add the chickpeas, onions, tomatoes, coriander leaves (cilantro), turmeric, ginger and pepper.

2. Simmer over low heat for 1 hour until the meat is tender and the chickpeas soft.

3. Add the rice vermicelli and tomato purée (tomato paste) and boil until the vermicelli is soft. Season with salt.

4. Just before serving, garnish with parsley.

Note: This soup may be thickened by adding 1 tablespoon plain (all-purpose) flour mixed with 2 tablespoons water while boiling.

CLAM SOUP

Ingredients

1 tablespoon olive oil

3 cloves garlic, peeled and finely chopped

2 tomatoes, finely chopped

1 bird's eye chilli, finely chopped

300 grams/10$\frac{1}{2}$ ounces clams

500 ml/16 fl oz/2 cups fish stock

1 stalk lemon grass, bruised

coriander leaves (cilantro), chopped

Method

1. Heat the oil in a soup pot and sauté the garlic and tomatoes until soft.

2. Add the chilli, clams, fish stock and lemon grass. Cover the pot and boil for 5 minutes.

3. Just before serving, garnish with coriander leaves (cilantro).

SOTO KUDUS
(Spicy Chicken Soup)

Ingredients

cooking oil for deep-frying + 3 tablespoons

500 grams/1 pound, 1½ ounces
   potatoes, peeled and finely sliced
   into rounds

1 (1 kilogram/2 pounds, 3 ounces) chicken

1.25 litres/2 pints/5 cups water

2 stalks lemon grass, bruised

2 cm/1 inch galangal, peeled and bruised

3 *salam* leaves

90 grams/3 ounces/2 cups glass noodles,
   blanched just before serving

200 grams/7 ounces bean sprouts,
   blanched just before serving

3 eggs, hard-boiled, shelled and cut
   into rounds or wedges

Spicy Bird's Eye Chilli Sauce*

coriander leaves (cilantro), chopped

crisp-fried shallots

sweet soy sauce

Finely Pounded Paste

1 teaspoon white peppercorns

5 candlenuts

2 cm/1 inch fresh turmeric, peeled

6 cloves garlic, peeled

Method

1. Heat the oil and deep-fry the potatoes until golden brown. Drain and set aside.

2. Boil the chicken in water until tender. Drain and briefly deep-fry it. Shred the meat. Set aside the chicken stock.

3. Heat 3 tablespoons oil and sauté the finely pounded paste with the lemon grass, galangal and *salam* leaves until fragrant. Add into the chicken stock and bring the soup to a boil.

How to Serve

1. In individual serving bowls, put fried potatoes, glass noodles, bean sprouts, eggs and shredded chicken. Pour chicken stock over.

2. Serve with Spicy Bird's Eye Chilli Sauce, coriander leaves (cilantro), crisp-fried shallots and soy sauce.

*SPICY BIRD'S EYE CHILLI SAUCE

Ingredients

10 bird's eye chillies, pounded

60 ml/2 fl oz/¼ cup dark soy sauce

60 ml/2 fl oz/¼ cup water

juice of 4 *kalamansi*

Method

1. Put the chillies, soy sauce and water into a pot and cook until thick.

2. Transfer to a bowl, add the *kalamansi* juice and mix well.

WANTAN SOUP WITH JAPANESE BEAN CURD

Ingredients

3 tablespoons corn oil

6 cloves garlic, peeled and finely chopped

½ carrot, peeled and finely diced

½ green capsicum (bell pepper),
   finely diced

½ red capsicum (bell pepper), finely diced

1.5 litres/2⅖ pints/6 cups water

1 chicken stock cube

10 cylindrical pieces Japanese bean curd,
   cut into rounds

Wantan Dumplings*

salt

freshly cracked black pepper

spring onion (scallion), chopped

coriander leaves (cilantro), chopped

Method

1. Heat the oil in a soup pot and sauté the garlic until fragrant. Add the carrot, green and red capsicums (bell peppers) and water together with the chicken stock cube. Bring to a boil.

2. Add the bean curd and Wantan Dumplings and simmer for 15 minutes over medium heat. Season with salt and pepper.

3. Just before serving, garnish with spring onion (scallion) and coriander leaves (cilantro).

*WANTAN DUMPLINGS

Ingredients

300 grams/10½ ounces prawns
   (shrimps), shelled, deveined,
   boiled and pounded

1 tablespoon *nam pla*

1 red chilli, finely chopped

2 spring onions (scallions), sliced

pinch of sugar

½ teaspoon ground white pepper

20 pieces ready-to-use wantan pastries

1 teaspoon cornflour (cornstarch),
   mixed with 2 teaspoons water

Method

1. To prepare the filling, thoroughly combine the pounded prawns (shrimps), *nam pla*, chilli, spring onions (scallions), sugar and pepper.

2. Put 1 teaspoon filling on a wantan pastries, wrap and secure with cornflour (cornstarch) mixture. Repeat with the remaining filling and wantan pastries.

Opposite: Wantan Soup with Japanese Bean Curd.

RICE & PORRIDGE

RICE & PORRIDGE

Rice forms the backbone of most Asian cuisines; it is the centrepiece of every meal. It is also the staple crop of more than half the world's population, with wheat as the next most important. Several people I've met swear that they can't go even a day without having a plate of rice!

My Chinese grandfather, who happens to be a fussy man, sometimes fusses over his meal when a bowl of rice is served to him. It has to be white, moist, fluffy and fragrant. He once told me that no day passes without a Cantonese—man, woman or child—having at least two bowls of rice, for unless a Cantonese eats rice at least twice daily, he or she will have no energy.

The rice eaten most widely today is the extra-long-grain variety, which is said to have been first cultivated in the area around Laos. Short-grain rice and glutinous rice, both popular in certain communities, are shorter in length than extra-long-grain rice and somewhat sticky when cooked. Brown rice is simply rice in which only the outer husk has been removed. In Singapore and Malaysia it is regarded as inferior—which, of course, we know is not the case—and is not popular except among some members of the Indian community. In the rest of the world it's popular among the health-conscious.

Aromatic varieties of long-grain rice are valued for their nutty flavour. The highly prized basmati, a thin rice grown in the foothills of the Himalayas as well as Pakistan, is essential to the traditional Indian pullao and biryani. It is often aged to improve its flavour and should be washed before cooking. Short-grain rice is used in most Japanese dishes. For sushi, it is mixed with rice vinegar. Spanish paella is traditionally made with long-grain rice, such as basmati. The most popular variety of Italian short-grain rice is arborio, an especially plump variety that can absorb sauce without turning too soft during extended cooking.

Within each type I've mentioned, the substitution of one variety of rice for another generally causes no problems, but long- or medium-grain rice should never be substituted for short-grain rice in a recipe, or vice versa.

All rice expands to at least twice its size when cooked. Although the end volume depends on the variety and the age of the rice, aged rice, which is especially appreciated in India, absorbs more liquid than freshly harvested grain. With the exception of basmati, rice need not be soaked before cooking unless stipulated in a particular recipe. All methods of cooking rice release starch, which can cause the grains to coagulate. Therefore, when a fluffy rather than a creamy texture is sought, some recipes may call for rinsing and draining the rice thoroughly after cooking.

The following rice recipes bring back wonderful memories of when I was a teenager preparing meals at Malay wedding banquets. Over the years, I have tried experimenting with new rice dishes as well as stealing ideas from other cooks at such events!

I've included in this chapter some of my very favourite congee (rice porridge) recipes. A popular convenience food cooked in many Chinese households, congee is also associated with convalescence. Ask any Chinese what he was fed as a child when he was ill, and chances are he'll tell you congee cooked with a little minced pork, chicken, beef or fish flavoured with all sorts of things. I have memories of myself having high fever or the flu and my mother giving me congee with fried anchovies, onions and peanuts along with sweet soy sauce. When my son, Mohd Nadzri, was six months old, I used to have fun experimenting with all sorts of delicious congee for him—until the doctor told me that he was overweight for his age!

Today we don't consume congee just when we are broke or sick. It's a wonderful light snack, even for the early morning hours, after three hours of dancing in a disco (as I've found!).

There are many eating establishments in Singapore and Malaysia that have come up with a wide menu of congee and accompanying dishes. Indeed, congee has long shed its association with the poor and sick and is now found in a variety of eateries. It can be cooked plain and eaten with a selection of dishes, or, as mentioned earlier, it can make a nutritious meal on its own with flavourful ingredients cooked into it.

Besides soup, congee is one of my favourite solutions for a quick meal when I'm alone at home. (My congee creations contain just about anything, from fish balls to sausages!)

JAMAICAN BEEF PILAF

Ingredients

- 55 grams/2 ounces/$\frac{1}{4}$ cup butter
- 3 shallots, peeled and finely chopped
- 3 cloves garlic, peeled and finely chopped
- 1 cm/$\frac{1}{2}$ inch ginger, peeled and finely chopped
- 1 cm/$\frac{1}{2}$ inch cinnamon stick
- 3 cloves
- 3 tablespoons meat curry powder
- 300 grams/10$\frac{1}{2}$ ounces beef strips, finely sliced
- 3 tablespoons dark raisins
- 2 green chillies, finely chopped
- 3 tomatoes, seeded and diced
- salt
- 450 grams/1 pound/2 cups basmati rice, washed and drained
- 250 ml/8 fl oz/1 cup coconut milk, extracted from $\frac{1}{2}$ grated coconut and 250 ml/8 fl oz/1 cup water
- 250 ml/8 fl oz/1 cup chicken stock
- 2 tablespoons chopped coriander leaves (cilantro)

Method

1. Melt the butter in a large, heavy pot and sauté the shallots, garlic, ginger, cinnamon and cloves until lightly coloured and fragrant.
2. Add the meat curry powder, stir for a few minutes and add the beef and raisins.
3. Add the chillies and tomatoes and season with salt.
4. Add the rice and stir for a few minutes before pouring in the coconut milk and chicken stock.
5. Add the coriander leaves (cilantro) and cook until the liquid is absorbed. Turn the heat low, cover and cook for about 7 minutes.

CRAB PILAF

Ingredients

- 300 grams/10$\frac{1}{2}$ ounces crabmeat
- 1 teaspoon salt
- 1 teaspoon ground black pepper
- juice of 1 lime
- 110 grams/4 ounces/$\frac{1}{2}$ cup butter or margarine
- 1 onion, peeled and finely chopped
- 2 cloves garlic, peeled and finely chopped
- 2 green chillies, finely chopped
- 2 tablespoons fish curry powder
- 2 tomatoes, diced
- 340 grams/12 ounces/1$\frac{1}{2}$ cups long-grain rice, washed and drained
- 750 ml/1$\frac{1}{5}$ pints/3 cups coconut milk, extracted from $\frac{1}{2}$ grated coconut and 750 ml/1$\frac{1}{5}$ pints/3 cups water
- 20 toasted almonds
- 1 carrot, peeled and sliced
- 2 sprigs coriander leaves (cilantro), chopped

Method

1. Marinate the crabmeat in salt, pepper and lime juice for 1 hour in the refrigerator.
2. Melt the butter or margarine and sauté the onion, garlic and chillies until soft. Add the fish curry powder and sauté for 3 minutes.
3. Add the tomatoes and fry for a few minutes. Add the rice, stir briefly and then pour in the coconut milk. Bring to a boil. Reduce the heat and cook until the rice is almost done.
4. Stir in the marinated crabmeat and almonds and cook until the rice is done.
5. Just before serving, garnish with carrot and coriander leaves (cilantro).

NASI HUJAN PANAS
(Coloured Chicken Rice)

Ingredients

- 55 grams/2 ounces/$\frac{1}{4}$ cup ghee
- 55 grams/2 ounces/$\frac{1}{4}$ cup margarine
- 1 cm/$\frac{1}{2}$ inch cinnamon stick
- 5 cloves
- 4 cardamoms
- 1 onion, peeled and sliced
- 2 cloves garlic, peeled and sliced
- 2 cm/1 inch ginger, peeled and sliced
- 2 tablespoons meat curry powder
- 500 grams/1 pound, 1$\frac{1}{2}$ ounces chicken fillet, cut into bite-sized pieces
- 1.25 litres/2 pints/5 cups water
- 2 tablespoons canned tomato sauce
- 55 grams/2 ounces/$\frac{1}{2}$ cup crisp-fried shallots + extra for garnishing
- 1.13 kilograms/2$\frac{1}{2}$ pounds/5 cups basmati rice, washed and drained
- 250 ml/8 fl oz/1 cup evaporated milk
- salt
- red, green and yellow food colouring
- 85 grams/3 ounces/$\frac{1}{2}$ cup cashewnuts, deep-fried until golden brown

Method

1. Heat the ghee and margarine and sauté the cinnamon, cloves, cardamoms, onion, garlic and ginger until fragrant.
2. Add the meat curry powder and chicken and stir well.
3. Pour in the water and add the tomato sauce and 55 grams/2 ounces/$\frac{1}{2}$ cup crisp-fried shallots. Bring to a boil and add the rice and evaporated milk. Season with salt. Cover and cook until the rice is done.
4. Sprinkle with food colouring and stir thoroughly.
5. Just before serving, garnish with crisp-fried shallots and cashewnuts.

BIRYANI

Ingredients

- 55 grams/2 ounces/$1/4$ cup ghee
- 2 stalks lemon grass, bruised
- 1 pandan leaf, shredded and knotted
- 4 tomatoes, finely chopped
- 2 tablespoons tomato purée (tomato paste)
- 435 ml/14 fl oz/$1^3/4$ cups chicken stock
- 125 ml/4 fl oz/$1/2$ cup evaporated milk
- 2 teaspoons saffron strands
- 400 grams/14 ounces/$1^3/4$ cups basmati rice, washed and drained
- salt
- 60 ml/2 fl oz/$1/4$ cup rose water
- raisins
- fried cashewnuts
- crisp-fried shallots
- mint leaves, chopped
- banana leaf

Whole Spices

- 3 cloves
- 3 cardamoms
- 1 star anise
- 2.5 cm/1 inch cinnamon stick

Finely Ground Paste

- 1 onion, peeled
- 8 shallots, peeled
- 2.5 cm/1 inch ginger, peeled

Method

1. Heat the ghee and sauté the whole spices, finely ground paste, lemon grass and pandan leaf until fragrant. Stir in the tomatoes and tomato purée (tomato paste).
2. Pour in the chicken stock and evaporated milk, add the saffron and bring to a boil. Add the rice and salt.
3. Cook until the rice is three-quarters done, sprinkle with rose water and cover with a piece of banana leaf. Cover the pot, reduce the heat and leave the rice to cook.
4. Garnish with raisins, cashewnuts, crisp-fried shallots and mint leaves.

NASI RAMPAI SELERA
(Mixed Fried Rice)

Ingredients

- 3 tablespoons cooking oil
- 225 grams/8 ounces shelled prawns (shrimps)
- 170 grams/6 ounces squid rings
- 1 carrot, peeled and diced
- $1/2$ celery stalk, diced
- $1/2$ red capsicum (bell pepper), diced
- 1.5 kilograms/3 pounds, $4^1/2$ ounces/ 8 cups cooked rice
- salt
- 85 grams/3 ounces/$1/2$ cup dark raisins
- 85 grams/3 ounces/$1/2$ cup cashewnuts, deep-fried
- 85 grams/3 ounces/$1/2$ cup almonds, deep-fried
- 3 spring onions (scallions), chopped

Finely Pounded Paste

- 6 shallots, peeled
- 5 cloves garlic, peeled
- 6 red chillies
- 1 teaspoon shrimp paste

Method

1. Heat the oil and sauté the finely pounded paste until fragrant. Add the prawns (shrimps), squid, carrot, celery and capsicum (bell pepper) and fry for 5 minutes.
2. Add the rice. Season with salt. Mix in the raisins and nuts and cook until the rice is heated through.
3. Garnish with spring onions (scallions).

LEMON AND MINT PILAF

Ingredients

- 140 grams/5 ounces/$5/8$ cup butter
- 1 onion, peeled and finely chopped
- 85 grams/3 ounces/$1/2$ cup almonds
- 2 fresh bay leaves
- 1 stalk lemon grass, bruised
- 2 stalks parsley, chopped
- 450 grams/1 pound/2 cups basmati rice, washed and drained
- rind of 2 lemons
- 560 ml/18 fl oz/$2^1/4$ cups chicken stock, or 1 chicken stock cube dissolved in 560 ml/18 fl oz/$2^1/4$ cups water
- 2 tablespoons chicken stock granules
- 4 tablespoons golden raisins
- 1 teaspoon salt
- 30 grams/1 ounce/$1/2$ cup chopped mint leaves
- 1 tablespoon lemon juice

Method

1. Melt the butter and sauté the onion, almonds, bay leaves, lemon grass and parsley until lightly coloured.
2. Add the rice and lemon rind and fry for a few minutes. Pour in the chicken stock and add the chicken stock granules, raisins and salt. Bring to a simmer. Add the mint leaves and lemon juice.
3. Cover the pot and transfer to a 180°C/350°F preheated oven. Bake for about 20 minutes. (Cooking by this method allows the rice to become light and fluffy.)

Note: This dish can also be cooked on the stove over low heat.

Opposite: Lemon and Mint Pilaf.

PAELLA VALENCIANA

Ingredients

- 60 ml/2 fl oz/¼ cup olive oil
- 6 cloves garlic, peeled and finely chopped
- 2 medium onions, peeled and finely chopped
- 2 fresh bay leaves
- 1 teaspoon chopped fresh thyme
- 1 heaped tablespoon paprika
- 2 celery stalks, finely diced
- 675 grams/1½ pounds/3 cups basmati rice, washed and drained
- 1 red capsicum (bell pepper), finely sliced
- 200 grams/7 ounces/1 cup green peas
- 1 can (411 grams/14½ ounces) Italian plum tomatoes, mashed
- 840 ml/1 pint, 7 fl oz/3⅜ cups seafood stock, or 1 chicken stock cube dissolved in 840 ml/1 pint, 7 fl oz/ 3⅜ cups water
- 1 teaspoon saffron strands
- salt
- freshly cracked black pepper
- 400 grams/14 ounces mixture of red snapper fillets, squid rings, prawns (shrimps) and clams
- 1 crab, halved
- 4 pieces chicken, cut into serving pieces
- 3 tablespoons chopped parsley

Method

1. Heat the oil in a paella pan and sauté the garlic, onions, bay leaves and thyme until fragrant.
2. Add the paprika and celery and stir-fry for 1 minute.
3. Add the rice and stir for 2 minutes. Add the capsicum (bell pepper), green peas, tomatoes, stock, saffron, salt, pepper, seafood and chicken. Stir well and bring to a boil.
4. Cover the pan with aluminium foil and cook over low heat until the liquid is absorbed and the rice is done.
5. Just before serving, garnish with parsley.

CHICKEN AND SEAFOOD JAMBALAYA

Ingredients

- 200 grams/7 ounces/⅞ cup butter
- 2 onions, peeled and chopped
- 4 cloves garlic, peeled and finely chopped
- 2 celery stalks, chopped
- 1 green capsicum (bell pepper), chopped
- 2 fresh bay leaves
- 1½ teaspoons salt
- 1½ teaspoons cayenne pepper
- 1½ teaspoons chopped fresh oregano
- 1¼ teaspoons ground white pepper
- ¾ teaspoon dried thyme
- 3 chicken breasts, diced
- 4 tomatoes, diced
- 180 ml/6 fl oz/¾ cup canned tomato sauce
- 500 ml/16 fl oz/2 cups prawn (shrimp) or seafood stock
- 450 grams/1 pound/2 cups long-grain rice, washed and drained
- 365 grams/13 ounces prawns (shrimps), legs and feelers removed
- 55 grams/2 ounces/½ cup chopped spring onions (scallions)

Method

1. Melt the butter and sauté the onions, garlic, celery and capsicum (bell pepper). Add the bay leaves, salt, cayenne pepper, oregano, white pepper, thyme and chicken and mix well. Add the tomatoes, tomato sauce and stock and bring to a simmer.
2. Add the rice and cook until the liquid is absorbed. Stir in the prawns (shrimps) and cook, covered, over low heat for 6–8 minutes.
3. Just before serving, garnish with spring onions (scallions).

NASI KERABU HIJAU
(Green Kerabu Rice)

Ingredients

- 3 mengkudu (morinda) leaves
- 6 pandan serani leaves*
- 2 pandan leaves
- 1 litre/1⅗ pints/4 cups water
- 450 grams/1 pound/2 cups fragrant rice, washed and drained

Method

1. Finely blend the mengkudu leaves, pandan serani leaves and pandan leaves with a little water in a blender. Squeeze out the juice and add more water to make 1 litre/1⅗ pints/ 4 cups.
2. Pour into a pot, add the rice and cook until done.

* A variety of pandan leaf that produces a more concentrated colour than the ordinary pandan leaf.

BUBUR MENADO
(Menado Vegetable Porridge)

Ingredients

675 grams/1¹/₂ pounds/3 cups jasmine
    rice, washed and drained
300 grams/10¹/₂ ounces tapioca, peeled
    and diced
2 stalks lemon grass, bruised
3 cm/1¹/₂ inches ginger, peeled and
    finely chopped
water
200 grams/7 ounces pumpkin, peeled
    and diced
3 ears corn; extract the kernels
300 grams/10¹/₂ ounces water
    convolvulus, roughly chopped
200 grams/7 ounces spinach, roughly
    chopped
handful of basil (*selasih*) leaves
Tomato Sambal*
fried or roasted salted fish
spring onion (scallion), chopped
Chinese celery, chopped
crisp-fried shallots

Method

1. Boil the rice, tapioca, lemon grass and
   ginger in water until half-cooked. Add
   the pumpkin and corn kernels and
   boil until the porridge is cooked. Add
   water as required during the cooking.

2. About 5 minutes before serving, add
   the water convolvulus, spinach and
   basil leaves.

3. Serve with Tomato Sambal, fried
   or roasted salted fish, spring onion
   (scallion), Chinese celery and crisp-
   fried shallots.

Note: For enhanced flavour, add 55 grams/2 ounces/
¹/₂ cup pounded fried dried prawns (shrimps) while
boiling the rice.

*TOMATO SAMBAL

Ingredients

5 red chillies
2 teaspoons roasted shrimp paste
2 tomatoes, finely diced
juice of 2 *kalamansi*

Method

Finely pound the chillies, roasted shrimp
paste and tomatoes. Stir in the *kalamansi*
juice.

CHEF WAN'S CHICKEN RICE

Rice

110 grams/4 ounces/¹/₂ cup margarine
2 onions, peeled and chopped
2 cm/1 inch young ginger, peeled and
    finely chopped
3 cloves garlic, peeled and finely chopped
1 cm/¹/₂ inch cinnamon stick
4 cloves
2 pandan leaves, shredded and knotted
900 grams/2 pounds/4 cups long-grain
    rice, washed and drained
1.4 litres/2¹/₅ pints/5¹/₂ cups chicken
    stock
salt

Chicken

1 (1.5 kilograms/3 pounds, 4¹/₂ ounces)
    chicken, halved
salt
freshly cracked black pepper
2 cm/1 inch ginger, peeled and pounded
2 cloves garlic, peeled and pounded
3 tablespoons sweet soy sauce
3 tablespoons margarine

Method

Rice

1. Melt the margarine and sauté the
   onions, ginger, garlic, cinnamon,
   cloves and pandan leaves until fragrant.

2. Add the rice and fry for a few minutes.
   Pour in the chicken stock and season
   with salt. Cook until the liquid is
   absorbed and then reduce the heat.

3. Cover and cook for another
   10 minutes.

Chicken

1. Rub the chicken with salt, pepper,
   ginger, garlic and soy sauce and then
   with margarine. Put it on a baking
   tray.

2. Bake in a 180°C/350°F preheated
   oven for 30–40 minutes until the
   chicken is cooked.

3. Cut the chicken into bite-sized pieces
   and serve with the prepared rice.

Opposite: Bubur Menado (Menado Vegetable Porridge).

LEBANESE CHICKEN RICE

Ingredients

- 1 (2 kilograms/4 pounds, 6 ounces) chicken, cut into 8 pieces
- 1 teaspoon powdered cinnamon
- 2 teaspoons ground black pepper
- 1 tablespoon allspice
- 1 tablespoon paprika or powdered chilli
- salt
- 60 ml/2 fl oz/¼ cup + 3 tablespoons olive oil
- 55 grams/2 ounces/¼ cup butter
- 85 grams/3 ounces/½ cup blanched almonds
- 3 onions, peeled and chopped
- 4 cloves garlic, peeled and finely chopped
- 3 cm/1½ inches cinnamon stick
- 6 cardamoms
- 2 fresh bay leaves
- 2 tablespoons tomato purée (tomato paste)
- 1 can (411 grams/14½ ounces) Italian plum tomatoes, mashed
- 1 litre/1⅗ pints/4 cups hot chicken stock
- 3 sprigs coriander leaves (cilantro), chopped
- 55 grams/2 ounces/¼ cup dark raisins
- 900 grams/2 pounds/4 cups basmati rice, washed and drained

Method

1. Marinate the chicken in cinnamon, pepper, allspice, paprika or powdered chilli and salt for 2 hours.
2. Heat 60 ml/2 fl oz/¼ cup oil and butter. Sauté the almonds over medium heat until golden. Drain.
3. In the same oil, fry the marinated chicken until three-quarters cooked. Remove and set aside.
4. Add 3 tablespoons oil and sauté the onions, garlic, cinnamon, cardamoms and bay leaves until the onion starts to caramelise.
5. Add the tomato purée (tomato paste), tomatoes and fried chicken. Cover and cook for 15 minutes over low heat.
6. Once the sauce starts to thicken, add the chicken stock and bring to a simmer.
7. Add the coriander leaves (cilantro), raisins and rice. Cook over medium heat, stirring periodically, until the liquid is absorbed. Cover, reduce the heat and cook for another 10 minutes.
8. Just before serving, garnish with fried almonds.

BUBUR KEMBOJA
(Cambodian Chicken Porridge)

Ingredients

- 60 ml/2 fl oz/¼ cup cooking oil
- 1 onion, peeled and diced
- 2 cm/1 inch ginger, peeled and finely sliced
- 3 cloves garlic, peeled and finely sliced
- 1 stalk lemon grass, finely sliced
- 30 grams/1 ounce/¼ cup dried prawns (shrimps), soaked in water, drained and pounded
- 1 (1.5 kilograms/3 pounds, 4½ ounces) chicken, cut into 8 pieces
- water
- 2 tomatoes, quartered
- freshly cracked black pepper
- 4 pieces dried radish, diced
- 2 tablespoons *tau cheo* (preserved soy beans)
- 450 grams/1 pound/2 cups Thai rice, washed and drained
- Sambal with *Kalamansi* Juice*

Condiments

- crisp-fried shallots
- lime wedges
- bean sprouts, tailed
- spring onion (scallion), sliced

Method

1. Heat the oil and sauté the onion, ginger, garlic, lemon grass and dried prawns (shrimps) until fragrant.
2. Add the chicken, enough water to cover it, tomatoes, pepper, dried radish and *tau cheo*. Cook until the chicken is tender. Remove the chicken, shred the meat and set aside.
3. Add the rice into the stock and boil until the porridge is cooked. Add water as required during the cooking.
4. Serve the porridge with the shredded chicken, condiments and Sambal with *Kalamansi* Juice.

*SAMBAL WITH KALAMANSI JUICE

Ingredients

- 4 red chillies
- salt
- juice of 1 *kalamansi*

Method

Finely pound the chillies and salt. Transfer to a bowl and mix in the *kalamansi* juice.

BUBURANEKA
(Rich Rice Porridge)

Ingredients

3 tablespoons ghee

3 cloves garlic, peeled and finely chopped

6 shallots, peeled and finely chopped

2 pandan leaves, shredded and knotted

2 star anise

5 cloves

5 cardamoms

2.5 cm/1 inch cinnamon stick

2 chicken breasts, finely diced

450 grams/1 pound/2 cups jasmine rice, washed and drained

100 grams/3½ ounces/½ cup dhal (split peas), soaked in water overnight and drained

85 grams/3 ounces/½ cup peanuts

1 carrot, peeled and diced

1 chicken stock cube, dissolved in 125 ml/4 fl oz/½ cup water

500 ml/16 fl oz/2 cups coconut milk, extracted from 1 grated coconut and 500 ml/16 fl oz/2 cups water

water

55 grams/2 ounces/½ cup *kerisik* (pounded roasted grated or desiccated coconut)

200 grams/7 ounces prawns (shrimps), shelled and deveined

salt

freshly cracked black pepper

coriander leaves (cilantro), chopped

Method

1. Heat the ghee and sauté the garlic, shallots, pandan leaves, star anise, cloves, cardamoms and cinnamon until fragrant.

2. Add the chicken and then the rice, dhal, peanuts and carrot.

3. Pour in the chicken stock, coconut milk and water. Boil until the porridge is cooked, adding more water as required.

4. Add the *kerisik*, prawns (shrimps), salt and pepper. Bring to a boil.

5. Just before serving, garnish with coriander leaves (cilantro).

Note: Sliced red chillies and spring onion (scallion) may also be used as garnishing.

NASI ULAM
(Raw Vegetable Rice)

Ingredients

500 grams/1 pound, 1½ ounces/ 2¼ cups rice, washed and drained

560 ml/18 fl oz/2¼ cups water

2.5 cm/1 inch fresh turmeric, peeled and finely pounded

2 pandan leaves, shredded and knotted

Fish Sambal*

200 grams/7 ounces bean sprouts, tailed

30 grams/1 ounce long beans, finely sliced

100 grams/3½ ounces cucumber, finely sliced

1 torch ginger bud, finely sliced

3 stalks *kesum* leaves, finely sliced

1 bunch *samak* (*Eugenia palembanica*) leaves, finely sliced

Method

1. Boil the rice with the turmeric and pandan leaves.

2. Just before serving, mix the cooked rice with the Fish Sambal, bean sprouts, long beans, cucumber, torch ginger bud, *kesum* leaves and *samak* leaves.

*FISH SAMBAL

Ingredients

100 grams/3½ ounces shallots, peeled

1 stalk lemon grass, finely sliced

½ teaspoon black peppercorns

½ grated coconut, roasted until crisp

1.25 cm/½ inch ginger, peeled

200 grams/7 ounces Spanish mackerel fillet, smoked over a low-heat charcoal fire and shredded

salt

sugar

Method

1. Finely pound the shallots, lemon grass, peppercorns, coconut and ginger.

2. Mix well with the shredded fish, salt and sugar.

Opposite: Buburaneka (Rich Rice Porridge).

MEAT

60

Daging Samak
(Grilled Beef Marinated in Spicy Sweet and Sour Sauce)

Stir-Fried Pineapple Beef

Hungarian Goulash

62

Pattaya-Style Chilli Fried Beef

Rendang Serai Riau
(Beef in Spicy Gravy)

Daging Badam Berempah
(Spicy Almond Beef)

64

Kerutup Daging
(Terengganu Beef Curry)

Rendang Dinding
(Beef Slices with Chilli and Soy Sauce)

Rendang Tok
(Perak-Style Beef Rendang)

66

Semur Daging Pontianak
(Pontianak-Style Sweet Soy Sauce Beef)

Beef with Bean Curd and Broccoli

Daging Bumbu Bali
(Balinese Spicy Beef)

68

Stir-Fried Ginger Beef with Asparagus

Daging Masak Asam Nanas
(Beef in Tangy Pineapple Sauce)

Dendeng Berlado
(Chilli Beef Slices)

70

Daging Puteri Manis
(Sweet Princess Beef)

Daging Kuzi
(Kuzi Beef)

Hawaiian Orange Teriyaki Steak

72

Opor Daging Hijau
(Beef in Rich Green Chilli Curry)

Pepper Steak

74

Mutton Dalca

Moroccan Beef Kefta

Stir-Fried Sesame Beef on Steamed Lettuce

76

Beef Moussaka

Daging Masak Hitam Cik Dah
(Beef Slices in Black Sauce)

78

Moroccan Lamb Shoulder

Texan Grilled Lamb Chops

Fruity Stir-Fried Lamb with Mango

80

Rissole Florentine

Stir-Fried Lamb with Leek and Onion

82

Provence-Style Grilled Lamb

Chutney-Glazed Lamb Chops

Nurjan Keema

84

BBQ Teriyaki Lamb Chops

Mutton (Lamb) Mysore

Dry Mutton (Lamb) Curry

For personal reasons, red meat is my least favourite food. When I was a child, I played with a baby goat that belonged to a friend. Almost every day I watched the goat feeding. It started by having its mother's milk, and a few months later it started eating grass. One day, after about 2 years later, when I went to visit it, it was not there any more. My father's friend told me that it was to be slaughtered the next day for an *aqiqah*. (*Aqiqah* is the slaughtering of a goat, sheep, cow, buffalo or camel on the seventh day after the birth of a baby as a form of thanksgiving to Allah.) I was in tears and couldn't sleep all night. The incident brought home to me how cruel we are to animals. It took me years to bring myself to eat a piece of meat. Of course, things have changed since then and I'm not vegetarian any more—but the memory still lingers in my mind. I hate going to the butcher; instead, I buy meat only at the supermarket. The sight of meat hanging from those hooks is too much for me … I suppose it's time to stop getting so personal, otherwise who's going to try out all these delicious recipes?

A general concern for health has popularised alternatives to red meat. Still, people have not turned away from red meat entirely, and it continues to be popular. Worries over the high fat content of red meat have been somewhat allayed by meat producers as they breed lean cattle and pigs. Meat is packed with nutrients such as protein, iron and zinc, and it therefore plays a vital role in a healthy diet. It is also the ideal source of a range of B vitamins—niacin, riboflavin and, to a lesser extent, thiamine. These vitamins are essential for the body to utilise the nutrients in food for energy production and the formation of red blood cells. Lean red meat (meat trimmed of visible fat) is called 'nutrient dense' by nutritionists, as it provides valuable nutrients but little fat or calories (kilojoules).

With dietary concerns allayed, people are glad to enjoy meat at the table and consumption is on the upswing once again. Beef, pork and lamb form the basis of many delicious meals. This is not to say that no changes have occurred. Instead of 350-gram/12-ounce steaks, the meat is more likely to be served in smaller portions, with vegetables and starches in a strong supporting or even equal role.

Before beginning to cook meat, a chef must learn to select high-quality meat and then handle it so as to maintain that quality. From personal experience, I have found that many home cooks have a poor understanding of the different cuts of meat as well as the cooking techniques required. As a result, the meat becomes dry and tough and loses its flavour. I know of someone who cooks a rendang using a filet mignon (*daging batang pinang*), thinking that since it's a prime cut the dish should turn out all right. Unfortunately, it doesn't.

So what should one look out for when buying meat? The quality of meat depends on what the animal was fed, the age at which it was slaughtered (whether it is a *lembu pencen* [retired ox] or not!) and how the meat was handled. Although the very best beef usually goes to restaurants and fancy butchers, it is possible to choose intelligently in a supermarket. As far as colour goes, look for bright pink or red flesh, light-coloured bones and creamy white fat. As for texture, look for fine flesh with a moist appearance. The flesh should not look grey and dull.

The best beef, the sort that is served at top-notch steak houses, has a delicate network of fat running through the flesh. This 'marbled' fat dissolves during cooking, providing automatic internal basting. Marbling is the key to the flavour and tenderness of meat. Veal (baby cow) and baby lamb have little marbling, but older lamb, and mutton to a lesser extent, should be streaked with fat.

Once the animal is cut, the meat is left to age so that the flavour develops and enzymes break down tough tissues, making the meat firmer, drier and more tender. The traditional method of ageing is to hang meat in an airy, moist atmosphere at a temperature of around 3°C/38°F. Unfortunately, storing meat in a home refrigerator does not improve its quality.

Once you decide on the dish you are going to prepare, if you are still confused by the different cuts laid in front of you, just ask your butcher for assistance. They know what to recommend. Tender beef, like tenderloin roast and steak, is cooked dry for short periods

M

E

A

T

of time (so *rendang Makcik* [aunt's rendang] is out), while tougher cuts like the chuck, round and brisket need slow, moist cooking (*OK-lah ini Makcik!* [This is it, aunt!]).

Cheaper and tougher cuts of meat can be tenderised in various ways, including cutting them thin, pounding and scoring. Marinating also helps to tenderise meat as well as enhance its flavour. Marinades may be wine based or simply a mixture of oil, spices, herbs or citrus juices like lemon and orange. During long marinating, juice is drawn from the meat, so the marinade may be used in the cooking. The following international recipes represent a wide range of techniques in preparing meat—stir-frying, pan-frying, grilling, stewing, roasting. The dishes are easy and practical and certainly enjoyable. I hope some of them will become your family's favourites in years to come.

DAGING SAMAK
(Grilled Beef Marinated in
Spicy Sweet and Sour Sauce)

Ingredients

- 400 grams/14 ounces beef, cut into 1.5-cm/$^3/_4$-inch cubes
- 1 teaspoon powdered fennel
- 1 teaspoon powdered coriander
- $^1/_2$ teaspoon ground black pepper
- 3 tablespoons ghee
- 3 cm/1$^1/_2$ inch cinnamon stick
- 4 cardamoms
- 3 cloves
- 2 star anise
- 1 cm/$^1/_2$ inch young ginger, peeled and finely pounded
- 4 cloves garlic, peeled and finely pounded
- 2 tablespoons powdered chilli
- 1 tablespoon tomato purée (tomato paste)
- 3 tomatoes, sliced
- 250 ml/8 fl oz/1 cup water
- 2 potatoes, peeled, diced and deep-fried until golden brown
- 3 tablespoons chopped coriander leaves (cilantro)
- salt
- sugar
- 125 ml/4 fl oz/$^1/_2$ cup natural yoghurt

Method

1. Rub the beef thoroughly with the fennel, coriander and pepper. Set aside.

2. Heat the ghee and sauté the cinnamon, cardamoms, cloves, star anise, ginger, garlic, chilli and tomato purée (tomato paste). Add the marinated beef and fry for 3 minutes.

3. Add the tomatoes and water. Simmer until the beef is tender.

4. Add the potatoes, coriander leaves (cilantro), salt, sugar and yoghurt. Simmer for another 5 minutes.

STIR-FRIED PINEAPPLE BEEF

Ingredients

- 3 tablespoons peanut oil
- 3 cloves garlic, peeled and finely chopped
- 0.5 cm/$^1/_4$ inch ginger, peeled and sliced
- 2 tablespoons hot bean paste
- 1 red capsicum (bell pepper), diced
- 2 tablespoons beef stock granules
- 500 grams/1 pound, 1$^1/_2$ ounces beef rump steak, finely sliced
- 2 tablespoons oyster sauce
- 125 ml/4 fl oz/$^1/_2$ cup plum sauce
- 2 teaspoons sugar
- salt
- freshly cracked black pepper
- 280 grams/10 ounces/2 cups diced pineapple
- coriander leaves (cilantro), chopped

Method

1. Heat the oil and fry the garlic, ginger and hot bean paste. Add the capsicum (bell pepper) and beef stock granules and fry until fragrant.

2. Stir in the beef. Add the oyster sauce, plum sauce, sugar, salt, pepper and pineapple.

3. Just before serving, garnish with coriander leaves (cilantro).

HUNGARIAN GOULASH

Ingredients

- 60 ml/2 fl oz/$^1/_4$ cup vegetable oil
- 4 large onions, peeled and sliced
- 1 teaspoon caraway seeds
- 1 teaspoon chopped marjoram
- 3 tablespoons paprika
- 1 kilogram/2 pounds, 3 ounces boneless beef chunk, cut into 2.5-cm/1-inch cubes
- 500 ml/16 fl oz/2 cups water
- 1 teaspoon cider vinegar
- 125 ml/4 fl oz/$^1/_2$ cup red wine (optional)
- 2 large carrots, peeled and cut into chunks
- 3 potatoes, peeled and halved
- salt
- freshly cracked black pepper
- 500 ml/16 fl oz/2 cups sour cream
- fettuccini pasta, cooked according to package instructions and drained

Method

1. Heat the oil and sauté the onions until soft. Add the caraway seeds, marjoram and paprika.

2. Add the beef and cook for a few minutes. Add the water, vinegar, red wine (optional), carrots and potatoes. Season with salt and pepper and cover.

3. Bring to a boil, reduce the heat and simmer for 45 minutes. Stir in the sour cream and serve with fettuccini.

PATTAYA-STYLE CHILLI FRIED BEEF

Ingredients

- 3 tablespoons peanut oil
- 10 shiitake mushrooms, soaked in water and finely sliced
- 500 grams/1 pound, 1½ ounces beef tenderloin, finely sliced
- 2 tablespoons oyster sauce
- 1 tablespoon sugar
- 3 tablespoons *nam pla*
- 1 onion, peeled and sliced in rounds
- ¼ green capsicum (bell pepper), diced
- ¼ red capsicum (bell pepper), diced
- 140 grams/5 ounces/1 cup canned sour bamboo shoots, sliced
- handful of basil (*selasih*) leaves
- 1 teaspoon cornflour (cornstarch), mixed with 1 tablespoon water
- spring onion (scallion), chopped

Finely Pounded Paste

- 4 red chillies
- 8 bird's eye chillies
- 3 cloves garlic, peeled

Method

1. Heat the oil and fry the finely pounded paste until fragrant.
2. Add the mushrooms and stir-fry until soft.
3. Add the beef, oyster sauce, sugar and *nam pla* and stir-fry for another 3 minutes.
4. Add the onion, green and red capsicums (bell peppers), bamboo shoots and basil leaves. Pour in the cornflour (cornstarch) mixture and stir for a few minutes.
5. Garnish with spring onion (scallion) and serve immediately.

RENDANG SERAI RIAU
(Beef in Spicy Gravy)

Ingredients

- 3 tablespoons cooking oil
- 1 litre/1⅗ pints/4 cups coconut milk, extracted from 1 grated coconut and 1 litre/1⅗ pints/4 cups water
- 2 stalks lemon grass, bruised
- 2 pieces *asam gelugur*
- 1 cm/½ inch galangal, peeled and bruised
- 300 grams/10½ ounces beef loin, finely sliced
- 10 medium prawns (shrimps), shelled and deveined
- 2 eggs, hard-boiled and shelled
- 1½ teaspoons salt
- sugar

Finely Ground Paste

- 10 red chillies
- 8 shallots, peeled
- 4 cloves garlic, peeled
- 8 candlenuts
- 1 cm/½ inch fresh turmeric, peeled
- 1 teaspoon powdered coriander
- 1 teaspoon powdered fennel

Method

1. Heat the oil and fry the finely ground paste until fragrant.
2. Add the coconut milk, lemon grass, *asam gelugur* and galangal. Simmer for 20 minutes until the gravy thickens.
3. Add the beef, prawns (shrimps) and eggs. Season with salt and sugar. Simmer for another 3 minutes until the beef is tender.

Note: Though rendang is usually dry, this dish has gravy.

DAGING BADAM BEREMPAH
(Spicy Almond Beef)

Ingredients

- 60 ml/2 fl oz/¼ cup cooking oil
- 900 grams/2 pounds beef tenderloin, cut into serving pieces
- 500 ml/16 fl oz/2 cups water
- 2 tablespoons tomato purée (tomato paste)
- 6 heaped tablespoons ground kurma spices
- salt
- 4 tomatoes, chopped
- 125 ml/4 fl oz/½ cup evaporated milk
- 100 grams/3½ ounces/⅝ cup ground almonds
- 2 tablespoons chopped mint leaves
- 125 ml/4 fl oz/½ cup natural yoghurt
- 300 grams/10½ ounces shallots, peeled, finely sliced and fried until crisp
- 45 grams/1½ ounces/¼ cup almonds, sliced and roasted

Finely Ground Paste

- 3 onions, peeled
- 4 cloves garlic, peeled
- 3 cm/1½ inches ginger, peeled
- 8 green chillies
- 4 red chillies

Method

1. Heat the oil and fry the finely ground paste until fragrant.
2. Stir in the beef. Add the water, tomato purée (tomato paste), kurma spices, salt and tomatoes. Bring to a simmer.
3. Add the evaporated milk, ground almonds, mint leaves and yoghurt. Stir thoroughly and add the crisp-fried shallots. Simmer until the meat is tender and the gravy thick.
4. Just before serving, garnish with roasted almonds.

Opposite: Pattaya-Style Chilli Fried Beef.

KERUTUP DAGING
(Terengganu Beef Curry)

Ingredients

125 ml/4 fl oz/$\frac{1}{2}$ cup cooking oil

2 onions, peeled and sliced

3 pandan leaves, shredded and knotted

1 kilogram/2 pounds, 3 ounces beef lean topside, finely sliced

750 ml/1$\frac{1}{5}$ pints/3 cups coconut milk, extracted from 1 grated coconut and 750 ml/1$\frac{1}{5}$ pints/3 cups water

2 pieces *asam gelugur*

salt

1 tablespoon sugar

55 grams/2 ounces/$\frac{1}{2}$ cup *kerisik* (pounded roasted grated or desiccated coconut)

1 turmeric leaf, finely sliced

Whole Spices

2 star anise

3 cardamoms

3 cloves

2 cm/1 inch cinnamon stick

Finely Ground Paste

20–30 dried chillies, seeded, soaked in water and drained

200 grams/7 ounces onions, peeled

4 cloves garlic, peeled

2 cm/1 inch ginger, peeled

2 tablespoons powdered coriander

1 teaspoon powdered fennel

1 teaspoon powdered cumin

15–20 black peppercorns

Method

1. Heat the oil and sauté the onions, whole spices and pandan leaves until fragrant. Add the finely ground paste and fry until the oil separates.

2. Add the beef and fry until it shrinks. Add the coconut milk together with the *asam gelugur*. Simmer until the gravy thickens.

3. Stir in the salt, sugar, *kerisik* and most of the turmeric leaf. Discard the pandan leaves and *asam gelugur*. Garnish with the remaining turmeric leaf and serve with ketupat or lemang.

Note: Traditional Kerutup Daging does not contain turmeric leaves, but I like the flavour they add.

RENDANG DINDING
(Beef Slices with Chilli and Soy Sauce)

Ingredients

250 ml/8 fl oz/1 cup + 3 tablespoons cooking oil

1 kilogram/2 pounds, 3 ounces onions, peeled and sliced

2 cm/1 inch ginger, peeled and grated

5 cloves garlic, peeled and sliced

100 grams/3$\frac{1}{2}$ ounces dried chillies, seeded, soaked in water and pounded

1 kilogram/2 pounds, 3 ounces beef rump steak, cut into 6-mm/$\frac{1}{4}$-inch thick slices

1$\frac{1}{2}$ tablespoons dark soy sauce

500–750 ml/16 fl oz–1$\frac{1}{5}$ pints/2–3 cups tamarind juice, extracted from 45 grams/1$\frac{1}{2}$ ounces tamarind pulp and 500–750 ml/16 fl oz–1$\frac{1}{5}$ pints/ 2–3 cups water

2 tablespoons sugar

salt

Method

1. Heat 250 ml/8 fl oz/1 cup oil and fry the onions, ginger and garlic for 5–7 minutes. Remove from the wok and grind coarsely.

2. In a clean pan, heat 3 tablespoons oil and fry the chillies. Add the beef and onion-ginger-garlic mixture.

3. Add the soy sauce and fry for 15 minutes.

4. Pour in the tamarind juice, add the sugar and salt and simmer over low heat until quite dry.

5. Serve with roti jala or rice.

RENDANG TOK
(Perak-Style Beef Rendang)

Ingredients

500 grams/1 pound, 1$\frac{1}{2}$ ounces beef topside, diced

1 litre/1$\frac{3}{5}$ pints/4 cups coconut milk, extracted from 2 grated coconuts and 1 litre/1$\frac{3}{5}$ pints/4 cups water

55 grams/2 ounces/$\frac{1}{2}$ cup *kerisik* (pounded roasted grated or desiccated coconut)

1 tablespoon powdered cumin

1 tablespoon powdered fennel

salt

sugar

Finely Ground Paste

4 tablespoons chilli paste

2 large onions, peeled

6 shallots, peeled

4 cloves garlic, peeled

3 cm/1$\frac{1}{2}$ inch ginger, peeled

4 stalks lemon grass, finely sliced

2 cm/1 inch galangal, peeled

Method

1. Put the beef, coconut milk and finely ground paste into a wok and bring to a simmer. Cook over low heat until the beef is tender.

2. Add the *kerisik*, cumin and fennel. Continue to simmer until the sauce starts to thicken.

3. Add salt and sugar and continue to cook until the beef is almost dry. Serve with rice.

Opposite: Kerutup Daging (Terengganu Beef Curry).

SEMUR DAGING PONTIANAK
(Pontianak-Style Sweet Soy Sauce Beef)

Ingredients

- 500 grams/1 pound, 1¹/₂ ounces beef, boiled and sliced
- 1 tablespoon + 4–5 tablespoons sweet soy sauce
- juice of ¹/₂ lime
- 60 ml/2 fl oz/¹/₄ cup cooking oil
- 5 shallots, peeled and finely sliced
- 3 cloves garlic, peeled and finely sliced
- 6 tomatoes, diced
- 750 ml/1¹/₅ pints/3 cups beef stock
- coriander leaves (cilantro), chopped

Roasted and Finely Ground Spices

- 2 teaspoons coriander seeds
- 1 teaspoon fennel seeds
- 1 teaspoon cumin seeds
- ¹/₂ star anise
- 3 cloves
- 10 black peppercorns
- 1.5 cm/³/₄ inch cinnamon stick
- 3 candlenuts

Method

1. Marinate the beef in 1 tablespoon soy sauce and lime juice for 30 minutes.
2. Heat the oil and sauté the shallots and garlic until fragrant. Stir in the roasted ground spices, tomatoes, marinated beef, 4–5 tablespoons soy sauce and beef stock.
3. Simmer until the beef is tender and the gravy thick.
4. Just before serving, garnish with coriander leaves (cilantro).

BEEF WITH BEAN CURD AND BROCCOLI

Ingredients

- 350 grams/12 ounces fresh beef rump, topside, blade or pre-cut beef strips
- 1¹/₂ tablespoons peanut oil
- 2 teaspoons peeled, finely chopped ginger
- 1 teaspoon peeled, finely chopped garlic
- 300 grams/10¹/₂ ounces broccoli florets, blanched in salted boiling water and drained
- 2 pieces hard bean curd, diced and deep-fried
- 2 teaspoons Shao Hsing wine or sherry (optional)

Marinade (blended)

- 1 teaspoon ginger juice
- 1 teaspoon Shao Hsing wine or sherry (optional)
- ¹/₄ teaspoon salt
- ¹/₂ teaspoon sugar
- 1¹/₂ teaspoons oyster sauce
- ¹/₂ teaspoon dark soy sauce
- ¹/₂ teaspoon sesame oil
- 1 teaspoon cornflour (cornstarch)
- pinch of ground white pepper

Sauce (blended)

- 1¹/₂ teaspoons oyster sauce
- ¹/₂ teaspoon dark soy sauce
- ¹/₄ teaspoon salt
- ¹/₂ teaspoon sugar
- ¹/₂ teaspoon sesame oil
- 1¹/₂ teaspoons cornflour (cornstarch)
- pinch of ground white pepper
- 60 ml/2 fl oz/¹/₄ cup chicken stock or water

Method

1. Slice the beef thinly across the grain.
2. Rub the marinade over the beef and set aside for at least 30 minutes.
3. Heat the oil and fry the ginger and garlic. Add the marinated beef together with the marinade and stir-fry for a few minutes.
4. Add the broccoli, bean curd and wine or sherry (optional). Pour in the sauce ingredients and bring to a simmer. Turn off the heat and serve immediately.

DAGING BUMBU BALI
(Balinese Spicy Beef)

Ingredients

- 125 ml/4 fl oz/¹/₂ cup cooking oil
- 500 grams/1 pound, 1¹/₂ ounces beef topside, cut into serving pieces
- 250 ml/8 fl oz/1 cup coconut milk, extracted from ¹/₂ grated coconut and 250 ml/8 fl oz/1 cup water
- 3 kaffir lime leaves
- 2 tablespoons dark soy sauce
- salt
- 3 tomatoes, quartered

Finely Ground Paste

- 5 candlenuts
- 8 red chillies
- 3 cloves garlic, peeled
- 1 cm/¹/₂ inch ginger, peeled
- 1 teaspoon powdered turmeric

Method

1. Heat the oil and fry the finely ground paste until fragrant. Add the beef, coconut milk and kaffir lime leaves. Simmer until the gravy thickens.
2. Stir in the soy sauce and season with salt. Add the tomatoes and cook for another 5 minutes.

Opposite: Beef with Bean Curd and Broccoli.

STIR-FRIED GINGER BEEF WITH ASPARAGUS

Ingredients

- 500 grams/1 pound, 1¹/₂ ounces beef loin steak, finely sliced
- 3 tablespoons cooking oil
- 4 cloves garlic, peeled and finely chopped
- 3 tablespoons peeled and finely sliced young ginger
- 20 asparagus spears, halved
- 60 ml/2 fl oz/¹/₄ cup water
- 1 red chilli, seeded and chopped
- coriander leaves (cilantro), chopped

Marinade (blended)

- 1¹/₂ teaspoons cooking oil
- ¹/₂ teaspoon salt
- 1¹/₂ teaspoons oyster sauce
- 1 teaspoon peeled, grated ginger
- 2 tablespoons cornflour (cornstarch)
- 1 tablespoon beef stock granules
- 1 teaspoon Tabasco sauce

Method

1. Rub the marinade over the beef and set aside for 3 hours.
2. Heat the oil and sauté the garlic, ginger and asparagus.
3. Stir in the marinated beef and pour in the water. Stir-fry the meat quickly to maintain its tenderness.
4. Garnish with chilli and coriander leaves (cilantro) and serve immediately.

Note: Chopped spring onions (scallions) may be added to the garnishing.

DAGING MASAK ASAM NANAS
(Beef in Tangy Pineapple Sauce)

Ingredients

- 125 ml/4 fl oz/¹/₂ cup cooking oil
- 1 kilogram/2 pounds, 3 ounces beef, cut into serving pieces
- 180 ml/6 fl oz/³/₄ cup tamarind juice, extracted from 2 tablespoons tamarind pulp and 180 ml/6 fl oz/ ³/₄ cup water
- 1 stalk lemon grass, bruised
- 1 cm/¹/₂ inch galangal, peeled and bruised
- 3 kaffir lime leaves
- salt
- sugar
- ¹/₂ pineapple, sliced

Finely Ground Paste

- 1 tablespoon coriander seeds, roasted
- 15 dried chillies, seeded, soaked in water and drained
- 2 onions, peeled
- 2.5 cm/1 inch ginger, peeled
- 2.5 cm/1 inch fresh turmeric, peeled
- 2 tablespoons shrimp paste

Method

1. Heat the oil and fry the finely ground paste until fragrant.
2. Add the beef and stir-fry. When the meat shrinks slightly, pour in the tamarind juice and add the lemon grass, galangal, kaffir lime leaves, salt and sugar.
3. Cook until the beef is tender and then add the pineapple slices. Stir well and simmer until the gravy thickens.

DENDENG BERLADO
(Chilli Beef Slices)

Ingredients

- 500 grams/1 pound, 1¹/₂ ounces beef lean topside, finely sliced and pounded flat
- 1 teaspoon ground white pepper
- 5 tablespoons sweet soy sauce
- cooking oil for deep-frying + 90 ml/ 3 fl oz/³/₈ cup
- 3 tablespoons vinegar
- salt
- sugar
- 2 onions, peeled and sliced in rounds

Finely Pounded Paste

- 10 red chillies
- 4 cloves garlic, peeled
- 1 cm/¹/₂ inch ginger, peeled

Method

1. Combine the beef slices, pepper and soy sauce. Deep-fry until crisp. Drain and set aside.
2. Heat 90 ml/3 fl oz/³/₈ cup oil and fry the finely pounded paste until fragrant.
3. Stir in the fried beef, vinegar, salt, sugar and onions. Serve immediately.

Opposite: Stir-Fried Ginger Beef with Asparagus.

...MANIS

Ingredients

...ee

...oves

3 sprigs curry leaves

3 cloves garlic, peeled and finely chopped

10 shallots, peeled and finely chopped

1 cm/^{1}/$_2$ inch ginger, peeled and finely chopped

4 tablespoons chilli paste

1 tablespoon powdered coriander

2 teaspoons powdered cumin

1 teaspoon powdered fennel

500 grams/1 pound, 1^1/$_2$ ounces fresh blade, knuckle or beef cubes

250 ml/8 fl oz/1 cup water

60 ml/2 fl oz/^{1}/$_4$ cup tamarind juice, extracted from 2 tablespoons tamarind pulp and 60 ml/2 fl oz/ ^{1}/$_4$ cup water

salt

2 tablespoons sugar

2 large potatoes, peeled, cut into wedges and deep-fried

2 large tomatoes, quartered

1 onion, peeled and sliced into rings

Method

1. Heat the ghee and fry the cinnamon, cardamoms, cloves and curry leaves. Add the garlic, shallots and ginger.

2. Add the chilli paste, coriander, cumin and fennel. Fry until fragrant.

3. Add the beef and water. Stir well and simmer for 30 minutes until the beef is tender and the sauce thick.

4. Add the tamarind juice, salt and sugar. Stir well before adding the potatoes, tomatoes and onion. Cook for another 2 minutes.

DAGING KUZI
(Kuzi Beef)

Ingredients

110 grams/4 ounces/^{1}/$_2$ cup ghee

3 tablespoons meat curry powder

2 pandan leaves, shredded and knotted

600 grams/1 pound, 5 ounces beef, finely sliced

3 tablespoons tomato purée (tomato paste)

250 ml/8 fl oz/1 cup natural yoghurt

250 ml/8 fl oz/1 cup water

85 grams/3 ounces/^{1}/$_2$ cup dark raisins

salt

sugar

30 grams/1 ounce/^{1}/$_4$ cup *kerisik* (pounded roasted grated or desiccated coconut)

coriander leaves (cilantro), chopped

Finely Ground Paste

10 dried chillies, seeded, soaked in water and drained

6 green chillies

6 red chillies

15 shallots, peeled

1 onion, peeled

1 cm/^{1}/$_2$ inch ginger, peeled

Method

1. Heat the ghee and sauté the finely ground paste with the meat curry powder and pandan leaves until fragrant.

2. Add the beef and tomato purée (tomato paste). Stir until the beef is almost tender.

3. Add the yoghurt, water, raisins, salt and sugar and simmer over low heat for 1 hour until the meat is tender and the gravy thick. Stir in the *kerisik*.

4. Just before serving, garnish with coriander leaves (cilantro).

HAWAIIAN ORANGE TERIYAKI STEAK

Ingredients

3 pieces (about 225 grams/8 ounces each) beef sirloin steak

tomatoes, grilled

fresh pineapple, sliced and grilled

Marinade (blended)

125 ml/4 fl oz/^{1}/$_2$ cup honey teriyaki sauce

2 tablespoons honey Dijon mustard

125 ml/4 fl oz/^{1}/$_2$ cup corn oil

2 tablespoons brown sugar

2 tablespoons peeled, finely chopped ginger

5 cloves garlic, peeled and finely chopped

2 teaspoons grated orange rind

125 ml/4 fl oz/^{1}/$_2$ cup orange juice

^{1}/$_2$ teaspoon cayenne pepper

Method

1. Rub the marinade over the beef. Put into a baking dish, cover and leave in the refrigerator for at least 5 hours.

2. Remove the beef from the marinade and pat it dry.

3. Heat the marinade over low heat until it becomes thick and syrupy.

4. Grill the beef over glowing charcoal to the desired doneness, periodically basting it with marinade.

5. Serve with grilled tomatoes and pineapple.

Opposite: Daging Puteri Manis (Sweet Princess Beef).

OPOR DAGING HIJAU
(Beef in Rich Green Chilli Curry)

Ingredients

125 ml/4 fl oz/½ cup vegetable oil

600 grams/1 pound, 5 ounces beef topside, diced

500 ml/16 fl oz/2 cups coconut milk, extracted from 1 grated coconut and 500 ml/16 fl oz/2 cups water

2 bunches pea eggplants

1 red capsicum (bell pepper), sliced

3 sprigs basil (*selasih*) leaves

salt

Finely Ground Paste

100 grams/3½ ounces green chillies

1 large onion, peeled

6 shallots, peeled

4 coriander roots

2 cm/1 inch ginger, peeled

2 stalks lemon grass, finely sliced

2 kaffir lime leaves

1 teaspoon shrimp paste

2 tablespoons coriander seeds, roasted

2 tablespoons fennel seeds

1 tablespoon white peppercorns

Method

1. Heat the oil and fry the finely ground paste until fragrant. Add the beef and cook, covered, for 5 minutes.

2. Pour in the coconut milk and bring to a boil. Simmer for 25 minutes. Add the pea eggplants, capsicum (bell pepper) and basil leaves and simmer for another 3 minutes.

3. Season with salt and serve with rice.

PEPPER STEAK

Ingredients

4 pieces (about 225 grams/8 ounces each) beef sirloin steak

salt

freshly cracked black pepper

3 tablespoons olive oil

2 shallots, peeled and finely chopped

3 tablespoons pickled green peppercorns, crushed

2–3 tablespoons Madeira, or 125 ml/4 fl oz/½ cup red wine or prune juice

375 ml/12 fl oz/1½ cups Brown Stock*

375 ml/12 fl oz/1½ cups cream

salt

2 tablespoons butter

Method

1. Season the beef with salt and pepper and grill or pan-fry to the desired doneness. Do not overcook it, otherwise it will be tough and dry instead of juicy. Set aside.

2. Heat the oil and sauté the shallots for a few seconds before adding the pickled peppercorns.

3. Add the Madeira or red wine or prune juice and reduce it.

4. Pour in the Brown Stock and simmer until it thickens. Add the cream and season with salt.

5. Turn off the heat and swirl in the butter to emulsify. Serve the sauce over the steak.

*BROWN STOCK

Ingredients

4–5 kilograms/8¾ pounds–10 pounds, 15 ounces veal bones

1 carrot, peeled and chopped

1 celery stalk, chopped

2 onions, peeled, grilled and chopped

2 tomatoes, chopped

1 leek, chopped

2–3 tablespoons plain (all-purpose) flour

1 tablespoon tomato purée (tomato paste)

few sprigs parsley

2 fresh bay leaves

1 teaspoon chopped fresh thyme

water

Method

1. In a roasting pan, mix together all the ingredients except water and roast at 200°C/400°F, stirring periodically, for about 1½ hours until the mixture browns.

2. Transfer the mixture to a large stock pot. Fill with water to cover the bones and simmer for 6–7 hours. Add more water during the cooking if necessary.

3. After 7 hours, the stock should be thick. Cool it for a few hours or overnight, partly covered, and then strain it.

Note: Leftover stock can be frozen for future use.

Opposite: Opor Daging Hijau (Beef in Rich Green Chilli Curry).

MUTTON DALCA

Ingredients

- 55 grams/2 ounces/$\frac{1}{4}$ cup ghee
- 45 grams/$1\frac{1}{2}$ ounces/$\frac{3}{8}$ cup meat curry powder, mixed with a little water to form a paste
- 1 kilogram/2 pounds, 3 ounces mutton (lamb) ribs, cut into bite-sized pieces
- 200 grams/7 ounces/1 cup dhal (split peas), soaked in water overnight and boiled until soft
- 1 litre/$1\frac{3}{5}$ pints/4 cups coconut milk, extracted from 1 grated coconut and 1 litre/$1\frac{3}{5}$ pints/4 cups water
- 1 eggplant, cut into 6 pieces
- 6 lady's fingers (okra), stemmed and halved
- 2 potatoes, peeled and quartered
- 1 large carrot, peeled and cut into 6 pieces
- 2 green chillies, halved lengthways
- 1 red chilli, halved lengthways
- 100 grams/$3\frac{1}{2}$ ounces long beans, cut into 3-cm/$1\frac{1}{2}$-inch lengths
- 2 tomatoes, sliced or quartered
- 60 ml/2 fl oz/$\frac{1}{4}$ cup tamarind juice, extracted from 1 tablespoon tamarind pulp and 60 ml/2 fl oz/$\frac{1}{4}$ cup water
- salt
- 6 shallots, peeled, sliced and fried until crisp

Finely Pounded Paste

- 10 shallots, peeled
- 2 cloves garlic, peeled
- 1 cm/$\frac{1}{2}$ inch ginger, peeled

Whole Spices

- 3 cardamoms
- 3 cloves
- 5 cm/2 inches cinnamon stick
- 2 star anise
- 4 sprigs curry leaves

Method

1. Heat the ghee and fry the finely pounded paste with the whole spices.
2. Add the meat curry powder and fry until fragrant.
3. Stir in the mutton (lamb) ribs and fry for a few minutes.
4. Add the dhal, coconut milk and all the vegetables and simmer for about 30 minutes.
5. Add the tamarind juice and season with salt.
6. Just before serving, garnish with crisp-fried shallots.

MOROCCAN BEEF KEFTA

Ingredients

- 700 grams/$1\frac{1}{2}$ pounds minced (ground) beef
- 2 large onions, peeled and finely chopped
- 4 cloves garlic, peeled and finely chopped
- 2 green chillies, seeded and chopped
- $\frac{3}{4}$ tablespoons powdered chilli
- 2 teaspoons powdered cumin
- 1 cm/$\frac{1}{2}$ inch ginger, peeled and finely chopped (optional)
- 6 sprigs parsley, chopped
- 2 tablespoons chopped coriander leaves (cilantro)
- salt
- freshly cracked black pepper
- 1 lemon, cut into wedges

Method

1. In a large bowl, thoroughly mix all the ingredients except lemon wedges.
2. Shape the mixture around metal skewers and grill, periodically rotating the skewers, over medium heat until the kefta is evenly cooked. Or pan-fry in a little olive oil until the kefta is cooked.
3. Serve warm with lemon wedges, accompanied by pilaf or pita bread and salad greens.

STIR-FRIED SESAME BEEF ON STEAMED LETTUCE

Ingredients

- 400 grams/14 ounces beef sirloin steak, cut into strips
- 1 tablespoon cooking oil
- 3 heads romaine or butter head lettuce
- 1 tablespoon roasted sesame seeds

Marinade (blended)

- 1 teaspoon ginger juice
- 2 teaspoons Shao Hsing wine or sherry (optional)
- 1 teaspoon sugar
- 1 tablespoon oyster sauce
- 1 tablespoon dark soy sauce
- $\frac{1}{2}$ teaspoon sesame oil
- 1 tablespoon ground black pepper
- 1 teaspoon cornflour (cornstarch)
- 1 tablespoon peanut oil
- salt

Method

1. Rub the marinade over the beef and set aside for about 3 hours.
2. Heat the oil and pan-fry the steak strips in a single layer for just 1 or 2 minutes on each side.
3. Meanwhile, boil some water in a steamer and steam the lettuce for about 2 minutes.
4. Arrange the lettuce on a serving dish and top with the fried beef. Sprinkle with sesame seeds. Serve immediately.

Opposite: Moroccan Beef Kefta.

BEEF MOUSSAKA

Ingredients

4 large round eggplants, cut into 1-cm/¹/₂-inch thick slices

salt

plain (all-purpose) flour for dusting

cooking oil for deep-frying

3 large potatoes, peeled and cut into 2-cm/1-inch thick slices

60 ml/2 fl oz/¹/₄ cup olive oil

2 large onions, peeled and chopped

1 tablespoon peeled, crushed garlic

500 grams/1 pound, 1¹/₂ ounces lean minced (ground) beef

1 teaspoon powdered cumin

1 can (411 grams/14¹/₂ ounces) Italian plum tomatoes, mashed

1 tablespoon tomato purée (tomato paste)

1 teaspoon chopped fresh thyme

1 tablespoon chopped fresh oregano

1 teaspoon ground black pepper

1 teaspoon sugar

1 green capsicum (bell pepper), sliced

Béchamel Sauce*

85 grams/3 ounces/³/₄ cup grated Parmesan cheese

Method

1. Arrange the eggplant slices in a single layer on a baking tray and sprinkle sparingly with salt. Set aside for 10 minutes to degorge.

2. Dab the eggplant slices dry with paper towels. Dust with flour and deep-fry in cooking oil until lightly golden. Drain and set aside.

3. Deep-fry the potato slices in cooking oil just until soft. Drain and set aside.

4. Heat the olive oil and fry the onions and garlic until soft. Add the beef and cumin and fry until lightly browned before adding the tomatoes and tomato purée (tomato paste). Add the thyme and oregano and simmer until the sauce thickens. Season with salt, pepper and sugar.

5. Put a little meat sauce at the bottom of a baking dish. Layer alternately with slices of eggplant, potato and capsicum (bell pepper). Ladle Béchamel Sauce on top and sprinkle generously with cheese.

6. Bake in a 180°C/350°F preheated oven for about 40 minutes until it starts to bubble and the top turns golden brown.

Note: The moussaka may be garnished with chopped fresh oregano before serving.

*BÉCHAMEL SAUCE

Ingredients

55 grams/2 ounces/¹/₄ cup butter

30 grams/1 ounce/¹/₄ cup plain (all-purpose) flour

500 ml/16 fl oz/2 cups hot milk

¹/₂ teaspoon ground nutmeg

salt

freshly cracked black pepper

Method

1. Melt the butter, stir in the flour and whisk quickly for about 1 minute. Stir in the milk and add the nutmeg. Simmer until the sauce thickens.

2. Season with salt and pepper.

DAGING MASAK HITAM CIK DAH
(Beef Slices in Black Sauce)

Ingredients

90 ml/3 fl oz/³/₈ cup cooking oil

1 kilogram/2 pounds, 3 ounces beef, finely sliced

3 pieces *asam gelugur*

45 grams/1¹/₂ ounces/¹/₄ cup brown sugar

1 litre/1³/₅ pints/4 cups water

125 ml/4 fl oz/¹/₂ cup sweet soy sauce

Finely Ground Paste

3 tablespoons powdered chilli or chilli paste

8 shallots, peeled

4 cloves garlic, peeled

2 teaspoons peeled, chopped ginger

4 stalks lemon grass, finely sliced

1 teaspoon powdered turmeric

Method

1. Heat the oil and sauté the finely ground paste until fragrant.

2. Add the beef, *asam gelugur*, brown sugar and water. Simmer until the beef is tender.

3. Stir in the soy sauce and cook until almost dry.

Opposite: Beef Moussaka.

MOROCCAN
LAMB SHOULDER

Ingredients

1 (800 grams/1³/₄ pounds) lamb shoulder, boned and trimmed

2 teaspoons powdered cumin

salt

freshly cracked black pepper

60 ml/2 fl oz/¹/₄ cup olive oil

3 onions, peeled and chopped

3 cloves garlic, peeled and finely sliced

1 carrot, peeled and diced

1 celery stalk, diced

1 teaspoon chopped fresh thyme

1 teaspoon chopped fresh rosemary

85 grams/3 ounces/¹/₂ cup whole blanched almonds, roasted lightly

250 ml/8 fl oz/1 cup dry red wine or prune juice

1 can (411 grams/14¹/₂ ounces) Italian plum tomatoes, mashed

1 teaspoon tomato purée (tomato paste)

110 grams/4 ounces/¹/₂ cup dried pitted prunes

110 grams/4 ounces/¹/₂ cup dried apricots

Method

1. Rub the lamb with the cumin, salt and pepper. Heat the oil and pan-fry the lamb over high heat. Set aside. Add the onions and garlic and sauté lightly.

2. Add the carrot, celery, thyme, rosemary and almonds and fry for 1–2 minutes before adding the wine or prune juice. Simmer until the gravy thickens.

3. Add the tomatoes, tomato purée (tomato paste), lamb, prunes and apricots. Cover the pan and transfer to a 180°C/350°F preheated oven.

4. Bake for about 40 minutes until the lamb is tender.

5. Just before serving, season with salt and pepper.

TEXAN GRILLED
LAMB CHOPS

Ingredients

8 lamb chops

500 ml/16 fl oz/2 cups tomato ketchup

125 ml/4 fl oz/¹/₂ cup cider vinegar

250 ml/8 fl oz/1 cup olive oil

90 ml/3 fl oz/³/₈ cup Worcestershire sauce

2 tablespoons brown sugar

1 tablespoon peeled, chopped shallots

2 tablespoons dark soy sauce

1 tablespoon chopped coriander leaves (cilantro)

125 ml/4 fl oz/¹/₂ cup water

Method

1. Thoroughly mix the lamb chops with all the other ingredients. Marinate for at least 8 hours.

2. Take the lamb chops out of the marinade and heat the marinade until thick and syrupy.

3. Grill the lamb chops evenly over glowing charcoal, basting periodically with marinade.

FRUITY STIR-FRIED
LAMB WITH MANGO

Ingredients

500 grams/1 pound, 1¹/₂ ounces lamb, cut into strips

60 ml/2 fl oz/¹/₄ cup cooking oil

2 red capsicums (bell peppers), diced

2 mangoes, peeled and diced

140 grams/5 ounces/1 cup diced pineapple

1 large onion, peeled and diced

freshly cracked black pepper

Marinade (blended)

¹/₂ teaspoon sugar

¹/₂ teaspoon salt

1 teaspoon peeled, finely chopped ginger

1 tablespoon oyster sauce

1 teaspoon sesame oil

2 tablespoons hoisin sauce

1 teaspoon cornflour (cornstarch)

2 tablespoons sherry (optional)

1 tablespoon Tabasco sauce

Method

1. Rub the marinade over the lamb and set aside for 3 hours.

2. Heat the oil and fry the marinated lamb.

3. Add the capsicums (bell peppers), mangoes, pineapple and onion. Season with pepper and more salt if necessary.

Opposite: Moroccan Lamb Shoulder.

RISSOLE FLORENTINE

This dish was on the Singapore Airlines dinner menu when I was flying from Singapore to Melbourne for one of my TV programmes. Although I came up with this recipe years ago, while living in San Francisco, I forgot how good the dish tasted. When I rediscovered it recently, I thought I must share it with you!

Ingredients

- 3 slices white bread, diced
- 60 ml/2 fl oz/$^1/_4$ cup milk
- 500 grams/1 pound, $1^1/_2$ ounces minced (ground) beef
- 2 egg yolks, beaten
- 1 onion, peeled and finely chopped
- 2 tablespoons chopped parsley
- 2–3 tablespoons olive oil + olive oil for shallow-frying
- 2 cloves garlic, peeled and finely chopped
- 300 grams/$10^1/_2$ ounces spinach, roughly chopped
- $^1/_4$ teaspoon nutmeg
- salt
- freshly cracked black pepper
- 110 grams/4 ounces/1 cup grated soft Swiss cheese
- plain (all-purpose) flour
- Tomato Sauce*

Method

1. Soak the bread in milk until soft and combine with the beef, egg yolks, onion and parsley.
2. Heat 2–3 tablespoons oil and sauté the garlic and spinach until the spinach wilts. Season with nutmeg, salt and pepper.
3. Take a handful of beef mixture, flatten it on your palm and fill with some spinach and a little cheese. Shape into ovals or round balls.
4. Roll in flour and shallow-fry briefly.
5. Transfer the rissoles to a baking dish and bake for 20 minutes in a 180°C/350°F preheated oven. Serve with Tomato Sauce.

Note: The dish may be garnished with chopped fresh parsley just before serving.

*TOMATO SAUCE

Ingredients

- 1 tablespoon olive oil
- 3 cloves garlic, peeled and chopped
- 1 onion, peeled and chopped
- 1 can (411 grams/$14^1/_2$ ounces) Italian plum tomatoes, mashed
- 2–3 tablespoons chopped parsley
- 1 teaspoon sugar
- salt
- freshly cracked black pepper

Method

1. Heat the oil and sauté the garlic and onion until soft. Add the tomatoes and parsley and simmer until the sauce thickens.
2. Season with sugar, salt and pepper.

STIR-FRIED LAMB WITH LEEK AND ONION

Ingredients

- 500 grams/1 pound, $1^1/_2$ ounces leg of lamb or pre-cut mini lamb steaks
- 2 tablespoons peanut oil
- 2 large leeks, cut into diagonal strips
- 1 large onion, peeled and cut into thick rings
- 2 red chillies, finely sliced
- 2 teaspoons peeled, finely chopped ginger
- 1 teaspoon sesame oil

Marinade (blended)

- $1^1/_2$ teaspoons peanut oil
- $1^1/_2$ teaspoons oyster sauce
- 1 tablespoon beaten egg white
- $^1/_2$ teaspoon ginger juice
- 1 teaspoon Shao Hsing wine or sherry (optional)
- $^1/_2$ teaspoon dark soy sauce
- $^1/_2$ teaspoon sesame oil
- pinch of salt
- 1 teaspoon sugar
- $^1/_2$ teaspoon ground white pepper
- $1^1/_2$ teaspoons cornflour (cornstarch)

Sauce (blended)

- $^1/_2$ teaspoon dark soy sauce
- $1^1/_2$ teaspoons oyster sauce
- $^1/_2$ teaspoon sugar
- 1 teaspoon cornflour (cornstarch)
- 3 tablespoons chicken stock or water
- pinch of ground white pepper

Method

1. Trim the fat off the lamb and slice the meat into thin strips. Mix it with the marinade and set aside for 30 minutes.
2. Heat 1 tablespoon peanut oil and stir-fry the leeks, onion and chillies. Remove and set aside.
3. Heat the remaining 1 tablespoon peanut oil and fry the ginger. Add the marinated lamb and stir-fry over high heat. Add the sauce ingredients and stir-fry for another 1 minute until the sauce thickens. Add the sesame oil together with the fried leeks, onion and chillies.

Opposite: Rissole Florentine.

PROVENCE-STYLE GRILLED LAMB

Ingredients

1 (2.5 kilograms/5 pounds, 7$\frac{1}{2}$ ounces) leg of lamb

salt

freshly cracked black pepper

1 tablespoon powdered chilli

1 tablespoon honey

3 tablespoons Dijon mustard

15 cloves garlic, peeled and halved lengthways

6 anchovy fillets

2 tablespoons fresh rosemary

few drops Tabasco sauce

2 onions, peeled and quartered

2 carrots, peeled and coarsely chopped

2 celery stalks, coarsely chopped

3 tomatoes, halved

60 ml/2 fl oz/$\frac{1}{4}$ cup extra virgin olive oil

juice of $\frac{1}{2}$ lemon

Method

1. Make 2-cm/1-inch incisions on the lamb. Rub the lamb with salt, pepper, chilli, honey and mustard. Push the garlic halves, anchovy fillets and rosemary into the incisions. Sprinkle with Tabasco sauce.

2. Grease a roasting pan with a little oil. Put in the onions, carrots, celery and tomatoes and top with the lamb. Sprinkle with oil and lemon juice.

3. Bake in a 200°C/400°F preheated oven for 1$\frac{1}{4}$–1$\frac{1}{2}$ hours until cooked. Remove from the oven and cover with aluminium foil for 15 minutes.

4. Carve and serve with baked potatoes and salad greens.

CHUTNEY-GLAZED LAMB CHOPS

Ingredients

8 lamb chops

Marinade (blended)

2 teaspoons powdered cumin

2 tablespoons powdered coriander

$\frac{1}{2}$ teaspoon paprika

$\frac{1}{2}$ teaspoon salt

60 ml/2 fl oz/$\frac{1}{4}$ cup extra virgin olive oil

Glaze (blended)

125 ml/4 fl oz/$\frac{1}{2}$ cup bottled sweet mango chutney

1 tablespoon red wine vinegar

1 tablespoon honey

2 cloves garlic, peeled and finely chopped

Method

1. Rub the marinade over the lamb chops and set aside for 1 hour.

2. Grill over medium heat, periodically basting the lamb with glaze.

3. Serve with green salad.

NURJAN KEEMA

Ingredients

500 grams/1 pound, 1$\frac{1}{2}$ ounces minced mutton (ground lamb)

1 tablespoon ginger paste

1 tablespoon garlic paste

125 ml/4 fl oz/$\frac{1}{2}$ cup cooking oil

2 tablespoons butter

200 grams/7 ounces Bombay onions, peeled and sliced

250 ml/8 fl oz/1 cup hot water

125 ml/4 fl oz/$\frac{1}{2}$ cup whipping cream

125 ml/4 fl oz/$\frac{1}{2}$ cup natural yoghurt

100 grams/3$\frac{1}{2}$ ounces tomatoes, quartered

100 grams/3$\frac{1}{2}$ ounces/$\frac{1}{2}$ cup green peas

1 green chilli, sliced

2 red chillies, sliced

1 leek, roughly chopped

salt

freshly cracked black pepper

85 grams/3 ounces/$\frac{1}{2}$ cup deep-fried cashewnuts

Whole Spices

2.5 cm/1 inch cinnamon stick

3 cardamoms

1 clove

Curry Paste (mixed well)

1 tablespoon garam masala

1 teaspoon powdered white pepper

1 tablespoon meat curry powder

2 tablespoons powdered chilli

1 tablespoon powdered cumin

1 tablespoon powdered coriander

60 ml/2 fl oz/$\frac{1}{4}$ cup water

Method

1. Heat a wok (without oil) and cook the mutton (lamb) with the ginger and garlic pastes for 3 minutes. Set aside.

2. In a fresh pan, heat the oil and butter and sauté the onion until it turns light brown. Add the whole spices.

3. Stir in the curry paste and fry for 5 minutes. Add the mutton (lamb) and hot water and bring to a simmer.

4. When the meat is tender, stir in the cream and yoghurt. Add the tomatoes, green peas, chillies and leek and simmer for another 3 minutes. Season with salt and pepper.

5. Just before serving, garnish with cashewnuts. Serve with bread or naan.

Opposite: Provence-Style Grilled Lamb.

BBQ TERIYAKI LAMB CHOPS

Ingredients

- 15 lamb chops
- 60 ml/2 fl oz/¼ cup light soy sauce
- 2 cloves garlic, peeled and finely chopped
- 2 shallots, peeled and finely chopped
- 1 cm/½ inch ginger, peeled and finely chopped
- 2 tablespoons lemon juice
- 125 ml/4 fl oz/½ cup any stock or sherry or red wine vinegar
- ½ teaspoon cayenne pepper
- 45 grams/1½ ounces/¼ cup brown sugar
- 1 tablespoon sesame oil
- 30 grams/1 ounce/¼ cup roasted sesame seeds
- ½ sprig coriander leaves (cilantro), finely chopped
- Pineapple Chutney*

Method

1. Mix the lamb chops with all the remaining ingredients except Pineapple Chutney. Marinate for a few hours in the refrigerator.
2. Grill over glowing charcoal and serve with Pineapple Chutney.

*PINEAPPLE CHUTNEY

Ingredients

- 1 tablespoon cooking oil
- 1 cm/½ inch ginger, peeled and finely chopped
- 1 clove garlic, peeled and finely chopped
- ½ teaspoon powdered turmeric
- 1 teaspoon mixed spice
- 250 ml/8 fl oz/1 cup water
- 225 grams/8 ounces/1 cup caster (super fine) sugar
- 125 ml/4 fl oz/½ cup cider vinegar
- 1 ripe pineapple, diced
- 1 red chilli, sliced lengthways

Method

1. Heat the oil and fry the ginger and garlic until fragrant. Add the turmeric, mixed spice, water, sugar and vinegar. Bring to a simmer.
2. Add the pineapple and chilli and simmer until the chutney is cooked.

MUTTON (LAMB) MYSORE

Ingredients

- 110 grams/4 ounces/½ cup ghee
- 3 onions, peeled and finely sliced
- 1 cm/½ inch cinnamon stick
- 5 cloves
- 5 cardamoms
- 3 star anise
- 3 stalks lemon grass, bruised
- 3 pandan leaves, shredded and knotted
- 4 cloves garlic, peeled and finely chopped
- 1 cm/½ inch ginger, peeled and finely chopped
- 500 grams/1 pound, 1½ ounces mutton (lamb), cut into large pieces
- 250 ml/8 fl oz/1 cup water
- 2 teaspoons powdered turmeric
- 2 tablespoons powdered chilli
- 2 tablespoons powdered cumin
- ½ tablespoon ground white pepper
- 250 ml/8 fl oz/1 cup tomato ketchup
- 60 ml/2 fl oz/¼ cup dark soy sauce
- 125 ml/4 fl oz/½ cup natural yoghurt
- salt
- sugar

Method

1. Heat the ghee and sauté the onions, cinnamon, cloves, cardamoms, star anise, lemon grass and pandan leaves until the onion is golden.
2. Add the garlic and ginger and sauté for another 2 minutes. Add the mutton (lamb) and water. Simmer

for 5 minutes. Add the remaining ingredients, stir well and simmer for 30 minutes until the mutton (lamb) is tender and the gravy thick.

DRY MUTTON (LAMB) CURRY

Ingredients

- 600 grams/1 pound, 5 ounces mutton (lamb), cut into bite-sized pieces
- 2 onions, peeled and coarsely sliced
- 250 ml/8 fl oz/1 cup natural yoghurt
- salt
- 60 ml/2 fl oz/¼ cup cooking oil
- 3 tablespoons tomato purée (tomato paste)
- 3 tomatoes, cut into rounds
- 5 tablespoons meat curry powder, mixed with 2 tablespoons water

Finely Pounded Paste

- 6 cloves garlic, peeled
- 1 tablespoon peeled, chopped ginger
- 1 green chilli
- 1 red chilli

Whole Spices

- 3 cm/1½ inches cinnamon stick
- 3 cloves
- 3 cardamoms

Method

1. Marinate the mutton (lamb) in the onions, yoghurt, salt and finely pounded paste for 15 minutes.
2. Heat the oil and sauté the whole spices until fragrant. Add the tomato purée (tomato paste), tomatoes and meat curry powder. Stir well.
3. Add the marinated mutton (lamb) and cook until the meat is tender and the gravy thick.

Opposite: BBQ Teriyaki Lamb Chops.

CHICKEN

98
Ayam Goreng Sri Wangi
(Fragrant Fried Chicken)
Kashmiri Chicken
Frango Piri-Piri

90
Moroccan Grilled Chicken
Ayam Goreng Jawa
(Javanese Fried Chicken)
Iranian Chicken Casserole

92
Honey Lemon Fried Chicken
with Spicy Pineapple Sauce
Lemon and Honeydew
Chicken
Ayam Panggang Bermadu
(Roast Chicken with Honey)

94
Vietnamese Chicken
with Mint
Green Chicken Curry
with Bamboo Shoots
Rendang Ayam Pedas
(Spicy Chicken Rendang)

96
Stuffed Chicken Meatballs
with Vegetables
Tandoori Chicken

100
Spanish Chicken Stew
Ayam Kapitan
(Chicken in Spicy Coconut Milk)
Ayam Goreng Tauco
(Fried Chicken with Preserved Soy Beans)

102
Gino's Baked Chicken
Chettinad Chicken

104
Chicken Kiev
Ayam Si Hitam Manis
(Chicken in Sweet Soy Sauce)
Ayam Dibulu
(Spicy Chicken Wrapped in
Banana Leaf)

106
Pencok Ayam Panggang
(Curried Roast Chicken)
Spicy Chicken Meatballs
with Lychee
Chicken Cacciatore

108
Opor Ayam Hijau
(Chicken in Green Curry)
Thai Fried Chicken Wings
Chicken Couscous

110
Sambal Goreng Hati Ayam
(Spicy Chicken Liver)
Kung Pao Chicken
Texan BBQ Drumsticks

112
Kerutup Ayam Kampung
(Kampung-Style Chicken Curry)
Pepes Ayam
(Chicken Wrapped in Banana Leaf)

114
Sambal Goreng Ayam Emak
(Mother's Chicken Sambal)
Steamed Ginger Chicken

Many of us can't get through a week of menu planning without including chicken at least once, and with good reason. It is inexpensive, versatile, easy to prepare and tasty. In this era of health-conscious dining, when almost everything that tastes good is supposedly bad for you, chicken can be eaten without too much guilt.

When you decide to cook chicken, there are many choices to be made. First, how do you cook it? Do you roast, grill, braise, bake, stir-fry or deep-fry it? What sort of seasoning do you use? The prospects are endless. In this chapter I've included more than thirty of my favourite recipes for chicken dishes from all over the world.

Eating chicken was, for some reason, a lot more fun when I was a kid. My favourite time was during school holidays, when my grandmother would make us chase a chook all around our compound before we finally managed to trap it. My grandmother said that whoever caught the chicken would get a drumstick, so my siblings and I were very strongly motivated. Now, dealing with the free-range chook is not so easy. They know our tricks. Unfortunately, most chickens today are raised in a confined area. But fortunately, they are available fresh or frozen all year round. So it is no longer necessary to know a 'hunter' to be able to enjoy them.

Chickens eat primarily corn and soy beans. These days they also receive vitamin and mineral supplements. Chicken is high in protein and low in calories and provides significant amounts of vitamins and minerals, including iron and vitamins A, B1 and B2. The highest concentration of these is found in the liver.

The fat in poultry is not marbled with the flesh as it is in beef or pork, but is instead mostly in or under the skin. Removing the skin before or after cooking cuts the fat content by nearly half. The breast and wings of the chicken constitute white meat, while the thighs and drumsticks constitute dark meat.

 CHICKEN

There are several types of chicken available in the market today, including broilers, fryers and roasters. Broilers and fryers are young chickens of either sex killed at six to eight weeks of age and weighing 1.13–2 kilograms/$2^1/_2$–$4^1/_2$ pounds. Traditionally broilers are smaller than fryers, but these days the terms are used interchangeably. They have tender flesh and can be prepared just about any way you wish. They are excellent grilled, fried or roasted.

Roasters can be of either sex. Young roasters are specially bred broiler-type chickens weighing 2.75–3.65 kilograms/6–8 pounds. Traditional roasters are a little older and weigh 1.59–2.28 kilograms/$3^1/_2$–5 pounds. The flesh of either type is tender, and as the name implies, roasters are very good roasted, rotisseried or cooked in liquid on the stovetop.

Chicken parts are also separately available in supermarkets today. Of course, chicken parts—like most other things that make life easier for us—are more expensive than whole chicken.

How to Buy and Store Chicken

Look for plump birds with smooth, unblemished skin, in secure packaging. When buying birds that are not packaged, buy them from a clean and reputable shop. Do not accept a bird that has changed colour or has an unpleasant odour. It should look slightly pink rather than grey, and it should be slightly warm if it has just been slaughtered. Chicken is highly perishable. Always check the 'sell-by' date on the package label.

When buying chicken don't plan to go anywhere after that—go home directly and refrigerate the chicken immediately. Never leave it in your car for more than 1 hour except in an ice chest. Chicken is difficult to keep fresh in a home refrigerator, so if you do not plan to cook it within two days of purchase it is wise to freeze it. Promptly discard raw chicken if there is even a hint of an odour. Rubbing plain (all purpose) flour or lime juice on chicken that has begun to spoil will never make it safe to eat. After handling raw chicken, be sure to wash your hands, countertops, cutting board and knives in hot, soapy water.

There has been much mention recently about the dangers of salmonella poisoning caused by eating chicken. Salmonella is an invisible, odourless bacteria that is widely prevalent in the environment. Any salmonella on chicken is destroyed when the internal temperature of the chicken reaches 140°C/275°F.

Following are some handy tips for preparing chicken dishes:

1. To sauté boneless chicken breast, brown it in about 3 mm/$^1/_6$ inch of fat. If less fat is used, the outside of the chicken will be dry and stringy and will not brown uniformly.

2. When preparing chicken for sautéing, use plain (all-purpose) flour, cornflour (cornstarch), an equal mixture of cornflour (cornstarch) and plain (all-purpose) flour, breadcrumbs or unsalted cracker crumbs to coat the chicken. This will keep the chicken from becoming dry and hard.

3. One of the best ways to cook chicken breast is to pan-fry it, then cover the pan and bake it in a 180°C/350°F preheated oven— about 15 minutes for breast with bone and 10 minutes for boneless breast. The chicken becomes succulent and tender, with an intense flavour.

4. Because white meat cooks faster than dark meat, when roasting or barbecuing chicken add breast meat 5 minutes after starting on the legs and thighs.

5. For roasting, use a shallow, heavy roasting pan that distributes heat evenly. Place the chicken on a non-stick wire rack resting on the rim of the roasting pan. This allows the hot oven air to circulate around the chicken and crisp the skin. Roast the chicken in a 230°C/450°F preheated oven. A hotter oven will cause the drippings to burn, while in a cooler oven the skin will not crisp. Since breast meat cooks faster than legs, add breast meat 5 minutes after you start to roast the legs.

6. Never stuff a chicken until just before roasting it, to prevent the growth of bacteria. However, the stuffing can be made hours ahead and refrigerated. Since stuffing expands during roasting, remember to stuff the chicken only three-quarters full so that it doesn't pop.

7. When sautéing boneless chicken breast, use an equal amount of butter and oil. Butter, which contains milk solids, browns during cooking to give the chicken a rich colour and an intense flavour.

8. Before braising or stewing chicken, it is important to season and dust the chicken pieces in plain (all-purpose) flour, preheat the pan until it is very hot and then sear the pieces a few at a time. The brown colour obtained through searing imparts a wonderful flavour to the dish. In addition, searing prevents the meat from drying out during the long process of cooking.

9. Grilling or barbecuing chicken is one of the tastiest and healthiest ways of cooking it. Barbecue over medium heat if the meat is thick, because it takes a longer time to cook. You can always finish cooking it in the oven. While barbecuing, make sure you baste the chicken often so that the meat stays moist and flavourful. Remember to stop basting 5 minutes before you remove the chicken, to avoid bacteria contamination from the marinade.

MOROCCAN GRILLED CHICKEN

Ingredients

1 (2 kilograms/4 pounds, 6 ounces) chicken, halved

salt

lettuce, torn into large pieces

cucumber, sliced

tomato, sliced

potato, boiled, peeled and sliced

lemon, cut into wedges

mint leaves

Chermoula Spice (finely ground)

3 red chillies

1 tablespoon powdered chilli

1 tablespoon paprika

1 teaspoon powdered turmeric

1 teaspoon powdered cumin

1 onion, peeled

4 cloves garlic, peeled

30 grams/1 ounce/$\frac{1}{2}$ cup chopped coriander leaves (cilantro)

60 ml/2 fl oz/$\frac{1}{4}$ cup olive oil

juice of $\frac{1}{2}$ lemon

Method

1. Rub the chicken with salt and chermoula spice and marinate for 3–4 hours in the refrigerator.

2. Remove the chicken from the refrigerator and let it come to room temperature.

3. Roast the chicken in a 180°C/350°F preheated oven for 45 minutes, turning it after 20 minutes.

4. Serve with lettuce, cucumber, tomato, potato, lemon and mint leaves.

AYAM GORENG JAWA
(Javanese Fried Chicken)

Ingredients

1 (1.5 kilograms/3 pounds, 4$\frac{1}{2}$ ounces) chicken, cut into serving pieces

375 ml/12 fl oz/1$\frac{1}{2}$ cups coconut milk, extracted from 1 grated coconut and 375 ml/12 fl oz/1$\frac{1}{2}$ cups water

60 ml/2 fl oz/$\frac{1}{4}$ cup tamarind juice, extracted from 1 teaspoon tamarind pulp and 60 ml/2 fl oz/$\frac{1}{4}$ cup water

salt

cooking oil for deep-frying

Finely Ground Paste

4 red chillies

2 teaspoons coriander seeds

2 candlenuts

12 shallots, peeled

1 stalk lemon grass, finely sliced

2.5 cm/1 inch galangal, peeled

2.5 cm/1 inch fresh turmeric, peeled

2 teaspoons grated palm sugar or brown sugar

Method

1. Thoroughly combine the chicken with the finely ground paste and all the other ingredients except oil. Simmer over medium heat until the chicken is tender and the gravy thick. Remove from heat. Separate the chicken from the gravy.

2. Heat the oil and deep-fry the chicken pieces until golden brown. Drain.

3. Serve the fried chicken with the reserved gravy.

IRANIAN CHICKEN CASSEROLE

Ingredients

1 (1 kilogram/2 pounds, 3 ounces) chicken, cut into 4 pieces

salt

freshly cracked black pepper

cooking oil for deep-frying

2 round eggplants, thinly sliced

4 tomatoes, halved

200 grams/7 ounces/1 cup drained canned chickpeas

3 tablespoons finely chopped coriander leaves (cilantro)

55 grams/2 ounces/$\frac{1}{4}$ cup butter

1 onion, peeled and diced

60 ml/2 fl oz/$\frac{1}{4}$ cup tomato purée (tomato paste)

375 ml/12 fl oz/1$\frac{1}{2}$ cups water

2 teaspoons salt

1 teaspoon saffron strands

1 tablespoon honey

Method

1. Rub the chicken with salt and pepper. Deep-fry until half-cooked and drain.

2. In the same oil, fry separately the eggplants and tomatoes until soft. Drain.

3. Arrange the eggplants, tomatoes and chickpeas in a roasting pan. Sprinkle with coriander leaves (cilantro) and place the chicken on top. Set aside.

4. Heat the butter and sauté the onion until soft. Add the tomato purée (tomato paste) and water. When the mixture boils, add the salt, saffron and honey and cook for another 2 minutes. Stir and pour over the chicken.

5. Cover the roasting pan with aluminium foil and roast in a 180°C/350°F preheated oven for 30–35 minutes.

Opposite: Moroccan Grilled Chicken.

HONEY LEMON FRIED CHICKEN WITH SPICY PINEAPPLE SAUCE

Ingredients

  8–12 pieces chicken
  cooking oil for deep-frying
  Pineapple Sauce*

Marinade (blended)

  juice of 1 lemon
  2 tablespoons honey
  1 tablespoon chopped coriander leaves
    (cilantro)

Batter (blended)

  2 tablespoons plain (all-purpose) flour
  45 grams/1^1/$_2$ ounces/^{3}/$_8$ cup cornflour
    (cornstarch)
  1 egg, beaten

Method

1. Rub the marinade over the chicken and set aside for 2–3 hours.

2. In a large bowl, combine the marinated chicken with the batter. Coat the chicken pieces very well before deep-frying until golden brown. Drain and arrange on a serving platter.

3. Serve with Pineapple Sauce.

*PINEAPPLE SAUCE

Ingredients

  110 grams/4 ounces/^{1}/$_2$ cup sugar
  375 ml/12 fl oz/1^1/$_2$ cups fresh
    pineapple juice
  60 ml/2 fl oz/^{1}/$_4$ cup white vinegar
  1 red chilli, chopped

Method

Put all the ingredients into a saucepan and simmer over medium heat until thick.

LEMON AND HONEYDEW CHICKEN

Ingredients

  4 boneless chicken breasts,
    cut into thin strips
  2 tablespoons oyster sauce
  1 tablespoon cornflour (cornstarch)
  2 tablespoons plain (all-purpose) flour
  1 egg, beaten
  85 grams/3 ounces/^{3}/$_4$ cup breadcrumbs
  cooking oil for deep-frying
  Lemon and Honeydew Sauce*
  1 red chilli, seeded and chopped
  lemon slice, cut into 6 pieces
  few strips lemon rind

Method

1. Marinate the chicken in oyster sauce and cornflour (cornstarch) for 15 minutes.

2. Dust the chicken pieces with flour. Dip them in beaten egg and coat with breadcrumbs. Deep-fry until golden brown, drain and arrange on a serving platter.

3. Pour Lemon and Honeydew Sauce over the fried chicken.

4. Garnish with chilli, lemon slices and lemon rind.

*LEMON AND HONEYDEW SAUCE

Ingredients

  85 ml/2^1/$_2$ fl oz/^{1}/$_3$ cup water
  85 ml/2^1/$_2$ fl oz/^{1}/$_3$ cup lemon juice
  60 ml/2 fl oz/^{1}/$_4$ cup honey
  2 teaspoons chicken stock granules
  2 teaspoons light soy sauce
  1 teaspoon lemon rind
  2 teaspoons cornflour (cornstarch)
  170 grams/6 ounces/1 cup honeydew
    melon balls

Method

1. Put all the ingredients except honeydew melon balls into a saucepan, and simmer until the sauce thickens.

2. Add the honeydew melon balls and heat through.

AYAM PANGGANG BERMADU
(Roast Chicken with Honey)

Ingredients

  2 chickens (1 kilogram/2 pounds,
    3 ounces each), cut into serving
    pieces, or 12 drumsticks

Marinade (blended)

  rind and juice of 1 lemon
  180 ml/6 fl oz/^{3}/$_4$ cup olive oil
  85 ml/2^1/$_2$ fl oz/^{1}/$_3$ cup honey
  1 tablespoon powdered fennel
  1 tablespoon paprika
  1 tablespoon powdered chilli
  6 cloves garlic, peeled and finely chopped
  4 shallots, peeled and finely chopped
  30 grams/1 ounce/^{1}/$_2$ cup chopped
    coriander leaves (cilantro)
  30 grams/1 ounce/^{1}/$_2$ cup chopped
    mint leaves
  ^{1}/$_4$ teaspoon powdered nutmeg
  2 teaspoons salt

Method

1. Thoroughly combine the chicken with the marinade. Refrigerate overnight.

2. Grill the chicken on an electric grill or in the oven.

Opposite: Lemon and Honeydew Chicken.

VIETNAMESE CHICKEN WITH MINT

Ingredients

- 600 grams/1 pound, 5 ounces chicken breast, cut into thin strips
- 60 ml/2 fl oz/¼ cup vegetable oil
- 3 stalks lemon grass, sliced
- salt
- sugar
- juice of 1 lime
- handful of mint leaves, chopped

Marinade (finely ground)

- 1 large onion, peeled
- 4 cloves garlic, peeled
- 1 cm/½ inch ginger, peeled
- 1 tablespoon *nam pla*
- 1 teaspoon ground white pepper

Finely Ground Paste

- 10 large red chillies
- 1 tablespoon shrimp paste
- 2 stalks lemon grass, finely sliced
- 1 cm/½ inch ginger, peeled
- 4 cloves garlic, peeled

Method

1. Combine the chicken with the marinade and refrigerate for at least 2 hours.
2. Heat the oil and fry the lemon grass for a few minutes. Add the finely ground paste and continue frying until fragrant.
3. Add the marinated chicken and fry until it is cooked through. Season with salt, sugar and lime juice. Just before serving, toss in the mint leaves.

Note: The dish may be garnished with kaffir lime leaves and shredded lemon grass.

GREEN CHICKEN CURRY WITH BAMBOO SHOOTS

Ingredients

- 3 tablespoons cooking oil
- 250 ml/8 fl oz/1 cup coconut milk, extracted from ½ grated coconut and 250 ml/8 fl oz/1 cup water
- 1 (1 kilogram/2 pounds, 3 ounces) chicken, cut into serving pieces
- 250 ml/8 fl oz/1 cup evaporated milk
- 70 grams/2½ ounces/½ cup fresh or canned bamboo shoots, sliced
- 2 red chillies, halved lengthways
- 3 kaffir lime leaves
- 3 tablespoons *nam pla*
- 1 sprig basil (*selasih*) leaves
- 3 tablespoons sugar

Green Curry Paste (finely ground)

- 2 green chillies
- 20 bird's eye chillies
- 1 tablespoon coriander seeds
- 1 tablespoon white peppercorns
- 1 teaspoon shrimp paste
- 7 shallots, peeled
- 7 cloves garlic, peeled
- 2 cm/1 inch galangal, peeled
- 1 stalk lemon grass, finely sliced
- 2 coriander roots, sliced
- rind of ⅓ kaffir lime

Method

1. Heat the oil and fry the green curry paste until fragrant.
2. Pour in the coconut milk, add the chicken and simmer until the chicken is almost tender.
3. Stir in the evaporated milk, then add the bamboo shoots, chillies, kaffir lime leaves, *nam pla*, basil leaves and sugar.
4. Simmer for another 5 minutes before serving.

RENDANG AYAM PEDAS
(Spicy Chicken Rendang)

Ingredients

- 1 (1.5 kilograms/3 pounds, 4½ ounces) chicken, cut into 12 pieces
- 500 ml/16 fl oz/2 cups coconut milk, extracted from 1½ grated coconuts and 500 ml/16 fl oz/2 cups water
- 55 grams/2 ounces/½ cup *kerisik* (pounded roasted grated or desiccated coconut)
- salt
- sugar
- 1 turmeric leaf, finely sliced

Finely Ground Paste

- 8 shallots, peeled
- 3 cloves garlic, peeled
- 3 stalks lemon grass, finely sliced
- 1 cm/½ inch ginger, peeled
- 1 cm/½ inch galangal, peeled
- 1 cm/½ inch fresh turmeric, peeled
- 5 bird's eye chillies
- 3 candlenuts
- 2 tablespoons chilli paste

Method

1. Combine the chicken with the finely ground paste and coconut milk and simmer for about 30 minutes until almost dry.
2. Reduce the heat and add the *kerisik*. Season with salt and sugar.
3. Add the turmeric leaf and give a quick stir before turning off the heat.

STUFFED CHICKEN MEATBALLS WITH VEGETABLES

Ingredients

- 3 tablespoons cooking oil
- 1 teaspoon peeled, chopped garlic
- 2 tablespoons peeled, chopped onion
- 1 teaspoon powdered chilli
- 55 grams/2 ounces/¼ cup button mushrooms
- ¼ carrot, peeled and sliced
- 1 tablespoon dark soy sauce
- 1 chicken stock cube, dissolved in 250 ml/8 fl oz/1 cup water
- 1 tablespoon cornflour (cornstarch), mixed with 2 tablespoons water
- Chicken Meatballs*
- 1 tomato, quartered
- 55 grams/2 ounces/¼ cup green peas
- ½ teaspoon salt
- 1 teaspoon sugar
- spring onions (scallions), chopped

Method

1. Heat the oil and sauté the garlic and onion until soft. Add the chilli, mushrooms, carrot and soy sauce. Pour in the chicken stock.
2. Add the cornflour (cornstarch) mixture and stir until the gravy thickens. Add the Chicken Meatballs, tomato and green peas. Season with salt and sugar.
3. Just before serving, garnish with spring onions (scallions).

*CHICKEN MEATBALLS

Ingredients

- 250 grams/9 ounces chicken fillet, minced (ground)
- 2 spring onions (scallions), chopped
- 2 tablespoons peeled, diced onion
- ½ egg, lightly beaten
- ¼ teaspoon salt
- 1 teaspoon sugar
- ¼ teaspoon freshly cracked black pepper
- 1 teaspoon cornflour (cornstarch)
- 8–10 quail eggs, hard-boiled and shelled
- cooking oil for deep-frying

Method

1. Combine all the ingredients except quail eggs and oil. Mix well.
2. With floured hands, shape the mixture into small balls. Place one quail egg in the centre of each ball and wrap the mixture around it.
3. Deep-fry the meatballs until well done. Drain.

TANDOORI CHICKEN

Ingredients

- 500 grams/1 pound, 1½ ounces chicken, skinned and cut into 4 pieces
- 2 tablespoons ghee
- lettuce, torn into large pieces
- tomato, sliced
- lime, cut into wedges
- onion, peeled and sliced

Marinade (blended)

- ½ tablespoon powdered chilli
- 1 tablespoon powdered turmeric
- ¼ tablespoon ground black pepper
- pinch of powdered clove
- 2 cloves garlic, peeled and finely chopped
- 1½ tablespoons lemon juice
- 1 tablespoon powdered fennel
- 1 cm/½ inch ginger, peeled and pounded
- pinch of powdered cinnamon
- pinch of powdered cardamom
- handful of mint leaves, finely chopped
- handful of coriander leaves (cilantro), finely chopped
- 60 ml/2 fl oz/¼ cup natural yoghurt
- 2 drops yellow food colouring

Method

1. Thoroughly combine the chicken with the marinade. Refrigerate, covered, for 5 hours.
2. Brush the chicken with ghee and grill it over glowing charcoal, turning periodically.
3. Serve with lettuce, tomato, lime and onion.

AYAM GORENG SRI WANGI
(Fragrant Fried Chicken)

Ingredients

    4 chicken breasts, skinned,
        boned and cut into strips
    cooking oil for deep-frying +
        1 tablespoon
    2 stalks lemon grass, finely sliced
    1 torch ginger bud, finely sliced
    10 bird's eye chillies, sliced
    2 tablespoons tom yam paste
    60 ml/2 fl oz/^{1}/$_4$ cup water
    1 teaspoon honey
    1^1/$_2$ tablespoons mayonnaise
    3 kaffir lime leaves, finely sliced

Marinade (blended)

    1^1/$_2$ tablespoons oyster sauce
    salt
    1 medium egg, beaten
    3 tablespoons cornflour (cornstarch)

Method

1. Combine the chicken with the
    marinade and set aside for 15 minutes.

2. Deep-fry the chicken until it is golden
    brown and crisp. Drain.

3. In a clean wok, heat 1 tablespoon
    oil and sauté the lemon grass, torch
    ginger bud, chillies and tom yam paste
    until fragrant.

4. Add the water, honey and chicken. Stir
    well. Remove from heat and stir in the
    mayonnaise. Add the kaffir lime leaves.

Note: This dish may be garnished with finely sliced
kaffir lime leaf.

KASHMIRI CHICKEN

Ingredients

    1 (1.5 kilograms/3 pounds, 4^1/$_2$ ounces)
        chicken, cut into 12 pieces
    125 ml/4 fl oz/^{1}/$_2$ cup natural yoghurt
    2 tablespoons tomato purée (tomato paste)
    110 grams/4 ounces/^{1}/$_2$ cup butter
    2 onions, peeled and finely diced
    2 cloves garlic, peeled and finely pounded
    1 cm/^{1}/$_2$ inch ginger, peeled and
        finely pounded
    4 cardamoms
    3 potatoes, peeled and diced
    60 ml/2 fl oz/^{1}/$_4$ cup water
    125 ml/4 fl oz/^{1}/$_2$ cup whipping cream
    handful of coriander leaves (cilantro),
        chopped
    2 green chillies, finely sliced
    salt

Curry Spices (mixed)

    2 teaspoons garam masala
    2 teaspoons powdered coriander
    1 tablespoon powdered fennel
    1 tablespoon powdered cumin

Method

1. Combine the chicken, curry spices,
    yoghurt and tomato purée (tomato
    paste) and marinate for 30 minutes.

2. Heat the butter and sauté the onions,
    garlic, ginger and cardamoms until
    lightly browned and golden.

3. Add the marinated chicken and cook
    for 5–7 minutes until the chicken
    shrinks a little.

4. Add the potatoes and water and
    simmer until the chicken is tender.

5. Stir in the cream before adding the
    coriander leaves (cilantro) and chillies.
    Season with salt.

FRANGO PIRI-PIRI

The Portuguese use a hot, Tabasco-like
sauce called *piri-piri* to spice up their
food. The potency of this home-made
sauce depends on the variety of chillies
used. Each home has its own traditional
recipe, but most of them have red
capsicum purée and vinegar among the
ingredients. Since *piri-piri* is not easily
available commercially, in this recipe
I have substituted it with Tabasco sauce.

Ingredients

    6 pieces chicken
    salt
    freshly cracked black pepper
    90 ml/3 fl oz/^{3}/$_8$ cup olive oil
    2 onions, peeled and sliced into rings
    4 red chillies, finely chopped
    3 cm/1^1/$_2$ inch cinnamon stick
    1 red capsicum (bell pepper), sliced
    1 yellow capsicum (bell pepper), sliced
    125 ml/4 fl oz/^{1}/$_2$ cup chicken stock
    1 carrot, peeled and julienned
    4 tomatoes, chopped
    1 teaspoon Tabasco sauce
    juice of ^{1}/$_2$ lemon

Method

1. Season the chicken with salt and
    pepper. Heat the oil and fry the
    chicken until golden brown. Drain.

2. In the same oil, sauté the onions,
    chillies and cinnamon until the onions
    are soft.

3. Add the fried chicken, red and yellow
    capsicums (bell peppers) and chicken
    stock. Simmer until the chicken is
    tender. Add the carrot and tomatoes.

4. Season with salt, Tabasco sauce and
    lemon juice.

SPANISH CHICKEN STEW

Ingredients

1 (1.5 kilograms/3 pounds, 4¹/₂ ounces)
   chicken, cut into 12 pieces

salt

freshly cracked black pepper

30 grams/1 ounce/¹/₄ cup plain
   (all-purpose) flour

60 ml/2 fl oz/¹/₄ cup olive oil

1 large onion, peeled and diced

1 carrot, peeled and finely diced

4 cloves garlic, peeled and finely chopped

1 teaspoon chopped (Western)
   basil leaves

1 teaspoon chopped fresh thyme

1 fresh bay leaf

1 red capsicum (bell pepper), diced

1 tablespoon tomato purée (tomato
   paste)

1 can (411 grams/14¹/₂ ounces) Italian
   plum tomatoes, mashed

500 ml/16 fl oz/2 cups chicken stock

10 button or shiitake mushrooms

10 green Spanish olives, pitted

10 black olives, pitted

1 teaspoon saffron strands

1 sprig parsley, chopped

Method

1. Season the chicken with salt and
   pepper. Roll in flour.

2. Sear the chicken in hot oil and drain.

3. In the same oil, sauté the onion, carrot
   and garlic. Add the basil leaves, thyme
   and bay leaf.

4. Add the capsicum (bell pepper),
   tomato purée (tomato paste),
   tomatoes and chicken stock and
   bring to a simmer. Add the chicken,
   mushrooms, green and black olives
   and saffron. Simmer until cooked.

5. Just before serving, garnish with
   parsley.

AYAM KAPITAN
(Chicken in Spicy Coconut Milk)

Ingredients

60 ml/2 fl oz/¹/₄ cup vegetable oil

1 (1.5 kilograms/3 pounds, 4¹/₂ ounces)
   chicken, cut into 12 pieces

500 ml/16 fl oz/2 cups coconut milk,
   extracted from 1 grated coconut and
   500 ml/16 fl oz/2 cups water

125 ml/4 fl oz/¹/₂ cup tamarind juice,
   extracted from 1 tablespoon tamarind
   pulp and 125 ml/4 fl oz/¹/₂ cup water

salt

Finely Ground Paste

20 dried chillies, seeded, soaked
   in water and drained

6 candlenuts

2 onions, peeled

15 shallots, peeled

4 cloves garlic, peeled

1 cm/¹/₂ inch fresh turmeric, peeled

1 cm/¹/₂ inch galangal, peeled

1 cm/¹/₂ inch ginger, peeled

3 stalks lemon grass, finely sliced

3 kaffir lime leaves

Method

1. Heat the oil and sauté the finely
   ground paste over medium heat until
   fragrant.

2. Add the chicken, stir well and cook,
   covered, for about 15 minutes.

3. Stir in the coconut milk and bring to
   a simmer, then add the tamarind juice.

4. Season with salt and cook until the
   gravy is slightly thick and the chicken
   tender.

AYAM GORENG TAUCO
(Fried Chicken with
Preserved Soy Beans)

Ingredients

4 chicken breasts, diced

60 ml/2 fl oz/¹/₄ cup peanut oil

85 grams/3 ounces/¹/₂ cup cashewnuts

2 red chillies, finely pounded

2 cloves garlic, peeled and finely pounded

1 cm/¹/₂ inch ginger, peeled and finely
   pounded

3 tablespoons *tau cheo* (preserved
   soy beans)

60 ml/2 fl oz/¹/₄ cup Shao Hsing wine
   (optional)

1 red capsicum (bell pepper), diced

1 yellow capsicum (bell pepper), diced

1 zucchini, finely diced

2 spring onions (scallions), finely sliced

handful of coriander leaves (cilantro),
   chopped

Marinade (blended)

2 teaspoons light soy sauce

2 teaspoons cornflour (cornstarch)

¹/₂ teaspoon sugar

Method

1. Combine the chicken with the
   marinade and set aside for 1 hour.

2. Heat the oil and fry the cashewnuts
   until golden. Drain.

3. In the same oil, sauté the chillies,
   garlic and ginger until fragrant. Add
   the *tau cheo* and marinated chicken.
   Cook until the chicken is tender.

4. Add the wine (optional), red and
   yellow capsicums (bell peppers)
   and zucchini and cook for another
   2–3 minutes. Toss in the fried
   cashewnuts.

5. Just before serving, add the spring
   onions (scallions) and coriander
   leaves (cilantro).

Opposite: Spanish Chicken Stew.

GINO'S BAKED CHICKEN

Gino Valente is a TV personality from Oslo, Norway. Although Italian, he and his gorgeous Norwegian wife have lived for many years in Asia. In 1998 we worked together on two TV series in Malaysia, which received high ratings during prime time in Oslo. I once witnessed Gino prepare this wonderful and simple chicken dish in less than 15 minutes. Together with this, he sautéed some green, red and yellow capsicums (bell peppers) with zucchini and baked some rosemary potato. We finished the meal with a delicious cantaloupe and home-made ice cream.

Ingredients

20 pitted Kalamata olives
3–4 anchovy fillets
4 cloves garlic, peeled
1 red chilli
handful of (Western) basil leaves
60 ml/2 fl oz/¼ cup extra virgin olive oil
6 boneless chicken breasts
salt
freshly cracked black pepper
30 grams/1 ounce/¼ cup plain (all-purpose) flour
2 tablespoons butter
60 ml/2 fl oz/¼ cup olive oil
125 ml/4 fl oz/½ cup white wine
fresh parsley, chopped

Method

1. In a small food processor, blend the olives, anchovy, garlic, chilli and basil leaves. Slowly incorporate the extra virgin olive oil to achieve a smooth paste. Set aside.

2. Make an incision in each chicken breast to form a pocket. Spoon some paste into the chicken breasts and fasten with a toothpick.

3. Sprinkle salt and pepper over the chicken breasts and dust with flour.

4. Melt the butter with the olive oil and pan-fry the chicken breasts on both sides, turning once during cooking. Transfer the chicken breasts to a serving platter.

5. Deglaze the pan with wine to form a sauce. Pour the sauce over the chicken breasts. Garnish with parsley.

Note: Sliced black olives may be added to the garnishing.

CHETTINAD CHICKEN

Ingredients

1 (1.5 kilograms/3 pounds, 4½ ounces) chicken, cut into 12 pieces
1 tablespoon + ¾ teaspoon powdered turmeric
1 teaspoon salt
cooking oil for deep-frying + 3 tablespoons
½ coconut, grated
2 onions, peeled and diced
4 sprigs curry leaves
2 cm/1 inch ginger, peeled and sliced
3 cloves garlic, peeled and finely chopped
2 tablespoons powdered chilli
¾ teaspoon garam masala
3 tomatoes, quartered
60 ml/2 fl oz/¼ cup water
salt
juice of 1 lime
handful of coriander leaves (cilantro), chopped

Lightly Roasted Spices

1 teaspoon fennel seeds
3 cm/1½ inch cinnamon stick
3 cardamoms
4 cloves

Method

1. Rub the chicken with 1 tablespoon turmeric and salt and deep-fry until golden. Drain.

2. Finely grind the coconut together with the roasted spices.

3. Heat 3 tablespoons oil and sauté the onions, curry leaves, ginger and garlic until fragrant and lightly browned. Add the ground coconut mixture, chilli, garam masala, ¾ teaspoon turmeric and fried chicken. Sauté for a few minutes.

4. Add the tomatoes and water and simmer until the gravy thickens.

5. Season with salt and lime juice.

6. Just before serving, garnish with coriander leaves (cilantro).

Opposite: Gino's Baked Chicken.

CHICKEN KIEV

This dish, which originated in Russia, was very popular in the United States in the 1960s and 1970s.

Ingredients

- 2 cloves garlic, peeled and finely chopped
- 15 grams/$^1/_2$ ounce/$^1/_4$ cup chopped parsley
- 140 grams/5 ounces/$^5/_8$ cup unsalted butter, softened
- salt
- freshly cracked black pepper
- 6 boneless chicken breasts
- 30 grams/1 ounce/$^1/_4$ cup plain (all-purpose) flour
- 2 eggs, beaten
- 110 grams/4 ounces/1 cup fresh breadcrumbs
- vegetable oil for deep-frying

Method

1. Make a paste of garlic, parsley and butter and season with salt and pepper. Chill for 20 minutes.
2. Using a meat pounder, pound the chicken breasts between 2 plastic sheets to about 0.5 cm/$^1/_4$ inch in thickness. Season with salt and pepper.
3. Place some garlic-butter paste on the chicken breasts. Roll and seal the edges together with a toothpick. Do it very carefully so that the chicken breasts stay intact.
4. Dust the chicken breasts with flour. Dip them in beaten egg and coat with breadcrumbs. Refrigerate, covered, for 1 hour.
5. Just before serving, deep-fry the chicken rolls until golden. Drain.
6. Remove the toothpicks and serve with vegetables.

AYAM SI HITAM MANIS
(Chicken in Sweet Soy Sauce)

Ingredients

- 1 (1.5 kilograms/3 pounds, 4$^1/_2$ ounces) chicken, cut into 12 pieces
- 1 teaspoon salt + salt for seasoning
- 1 teaspoon powdered turmeric
- cooking oil for deep-frying + 60 ml/2 fl oz/$^1/_4$ cup
- 15 dried chillies
- 10 shallots, peeled
- 5 cloves garlic, peeled
- 2.5 cm/1 inch ginger, peeled
- 2.5 cm/1 inch galangal, peeled
- 85 grams/3 ounces/$^1/_2$ cup dark raisins
- 85 ml/2$^1/_2$ fl oz/$^1/_3$ cup dark soy sauce
- 250 ml/8 fl oz/1 cup tamarind juice, extracted from 1 tablespoon tamarind pulp and 250 ml/8 fl oz/1 cup water
- 55 grams/2 ounces/$^1/_4$ cup sugar
- 2 pandan leaves, shredded and knotted
- 280 grams/10 ounces/2 cups diced pineapple
- 2 tablespoons chopped coriander leaves (cilantro)

Method

1. Rub the chicken with 1 teaspoon salt and turmeric. Deep-fry and drain. Reserve 60 ml/2 fl oz/$^1/_4$ cup oil and discard the rest.
2. In a clean wok, heat 60 ml/2 fl oz/ $^1/_4$ cup oil and briefly sauté the dried chillies, shallots, garlic, ginger, galangal and raisins. Grind in a blender until fine.
3. Fry the ground ingredients in the reserved oil until fragrant. Add the soy sauce, tamarind juice, sugar and pandan leaves. Season with salt and cook until the gravy thickens.
4. Stir in the fried chicken and pineapple. Season with more salt and sugar if necessary.
5. Just before serving, garnish with coriander leaves (cilantro).

AYAM DIBULU
(Spicy Chicken Wrapped in Banana Leaf)

Ingredients

- 3 chicken breasts, cut into serving pieces
- 3 chicken thighs, cut into serving pieces
- juice of $^1/_2$ lime
- $^1/_2$ teaspoon salt
- 3 tablespoons cooking oil
- 2 kaffir lime leaves, finely sliced
- 1 turmeric leaf, finely sliced
- 3 *salam* leaves
- banana leaves

Finely Ground Paste

- 10 shallots, peeled
- 2 cloves garlic, peeled
- 1 stalk lemon grass, finely sliced
- 1 teaspoon peeled, chopped ginger

Method

1. Rub the chicken with lime juice and salt and set aside for 30 minutes.
2. Heat the oil and sauté the finely ground paste until fragrant. Add the chicken and stir well.
3. Add the kaffir lime leaves, turmeric leaf and *salam* leaves.
4. Place 2 or 3 pieces of chicken on a piece of banana leaf, wrap and secure both ends with toothpicks. Repeat with the rest of the chicken.
5. Grill in a 180°C/350°F preheated oven for 25–35 minutes.

Opposite: Chicken Kiev.

PENCOK AYAM PANGGANG
(Curried Roast Chicken)

Ingredients

1 (1.5 kilograms/3 pounds, 4^{1}/$_{2}$ ounces)
   chicken

1 teaspoon salt

1 teaspoon ground white pepper

3 tablespoons cooking oil

435 ml/14 fl oz/1^{3}/$_{4}$ cups coconut milk,
   extracted from 1 grated coconut and
   435 ml/14 fl oz/1^{3}/$_{4}$ cups water

handful of basil (*selasih*) leaves

1 tablespoon tamarind juice, extracted
   from 1 teaspoon tamarind pulp and
   1 tablespoon water

salt

sugar

pineapple, chopped

Finely Ground Paste

4 red chillies

6 bird's eye chillies

4 candlenuts

8 shallots, peeled

2 cloves garlic, peeled

1 cm/^{1}/$_{2}$ inch galangal, peeled

Method

1. Rub the chicken with salt and pepper
   and grill in a 180°C/350°F preheated
   oven until half-cooked.

2. Heat the oil and sauté the finely
   ground paste until fragrant. Add the
   coconut milk and basil leaves and
   simmer for 15 minutes.

3. Add the grilled chicken and simmer
   over medium heat until the gravy is
   almost fully absorbed.

4. Add the tamarind juice, salt and sugar
   and cook for 3 minutes.

5. Just before serving, garnish with
   pineapple pieces. Serve with rice.

SPICY CHICKEN MEATBALLS WITH LYCHEE

Ingredients

600 grams/1 pound, 5 ounces boneless
   chicken breast

1 egg white

1 tablespoon cornflour (cornstarch)

^{3}/$_{4}$ teaspoon salt

^{1}/$_{4}$ teaspoon ground white pepper

110 grams/4 ounces/1 cup walnuts,
   finely ground

cooking oil for deep-frying

Lychee Sauce*

4 spring onions (scallions), chopped

Method

1. Finely grind the chicken in a food
   processor. Blend well with the egg
   white, cornflour (cornstarch), salt
   and pepper.

2. Shape the mixture into balls and coat
   with ground walnuts. Deep-fry the
   balls for 7 minutes. Drain and arrange
   on a serving dish.

3. Pour Lychee Sauce over the chicken
   meatballs.

4. Garnish with spring onions (scallions).

*LYCHEE SAUCE

Ingredients

1 can (565 grams/1^{1}/$_{4}$ pounds) lychees

170 grams/6 ounces/1 cup cantaloupe
   balls

60 ml/2 fl oz/^{1}/$_{4}$ cup Thai chilli sauce

juice of 1 orange

2 tablespoons cornflour (cornstarch),
   mixed with 2 tablespoons water

Method

1. Drain the lychees and reserve ^{1}/$_{3}$ of
   the syrup.

2. Pour the lychee syrup into a small pot
   with the lychees, cantaloupe balls,
   chilli sauce and orange juice. Bring to
   a boil.

3. Stir in the cornflour (cornstarch)
   mixture and cook, stirring constantly,
   until the sauce is thick.

CHICKEN CACCIATORE

Ingredients

1 (1.5 kilograms/3 pounds, 4^{1}/$_{2}$ ounces)
   chicken, cut into 8 pieces

salt

freshly cracked black pepper

3 tablespoons plain (all-purpose) flour

60 ml/2 fl oz/^{1}/$_{4}$ cup olive oil

1 onion, peeled and diced

4 cloves garlic, peeled and chopped

400 grams/14 ounces/2 cups button
   mushrooms, sliced

1 can (411 grams/14^{1}/$_{2}$ ounces) Italian
   plum tomatoes, mashed

1 tablespoon chopped parsley

500 ml/16 fl oz/2 cups chicken stock

Method

1. Rub the chicken with salt and pepper
   and coat with flour.

2. Heat the oil and fry the chicken until
   golden brown. Drain.

3. Reserve 3 tablespoons oil and discard
   the rest. In the reserved oil, sauté the
   onion and garlic until fragrant and add
   the mushrooms.

4. Stir in the fried chicken, tomatoes,
   parsley, chicken stock, salt and pepper.

5. Simmer for 20 minutes until the gravy
   thickens.

Opposite: Pencok Ayam Panggang (Curried Roast Chicken).

OPOR AYAM HIJAU
(Chicken in Green Curry)

Ingredients

    3 tablespoons cooking oil
    1 (1.5 kilograms/3 pounds, $4^1/_2$ ounces)
        chicken, cut into 12 pieces
    500 ml/16 fl oz/2 cups coconut milk,
        extracted from 1 grated coconut
        and 500 ml/16 fl oz/2 cups water
    250 ml/8 fl oz/1 cup water
    2 eggplants, cut into small pieces
        and deep-fried
    salt
    sugar
    handful of basil (*selasih*) leaves

Finely Ground Paste

    8 green chillies
    1 onion, peeled
    10 shallots, peeled
    4 coriander roots
    2 cm/1 inch ginger, peeled
    2 stalks lemon grass, finely sliced
    2 kaffir lime leaves
    1 teaspoon shrimp paste
    2 tablespoons coriander seeds, roasted
    2 tablespoons fennel seeds, roasted
    1 tablespoon white peppercorns, roasted

Method

1. Heat the oil and sauté the finely
    ground paste until fragrant. Add the
    chicken pieces and cook until they
    shrink.
2. Pour in the coconut milk and water
    and simmer until the chicken is tender
    and the gravy thick.
3. Stir in the eggplants. Season with salt
    and sugar. Add the basil leaves and
    remove from heat.

THAI FRIED CHICKEN WINGS

Ingredients

    15 chicken wings
    cooking oil for deep-frying

Marinade (blended)

    $^1/_2$ teaspoon lime juice
    2 tablespoons powdered coriander
    3 cloves garlic, peeled and finely chopped
    1 stalk lemon grass, pounded
    2 kaffir lime leaves, pounded
    1 teaspoon white peppercorns, finely
        ground
    $2^1/_2$ teaspoons *nam pla*
    1 tablespoon sweet soy sauce

Method

1. Combine the chicken wings with the
    marinade and set aside for at least
    1 hour or overnight.
2. Deep-fry the chicken wings until
    golden. Drain and serve immediately.

CHICKEN COUSCOUS

Ingredients

    110 grams/4 ounces/$^1/_2$ cup butter
    3 onions, peeled and finely diced
    2 cloves garlic, peeled and finely chopped
    1 (1.5 kilograms/3 pounds, $4^1/_2$ ounces)
        chicken, cut into 8 pieces
    1 tablespoon paprika
    2 teaspoons powdered fennel
    1 teaspoon powdered turmeric
    500 ml/16 fl oz/2 cups water
    1 tablespoon ground black pepper
    85 grams/3 ounces/$^1/_2$ cup chickpeas,
        soaked in water overnight and boiled
    2 round eggplants, quartered

    1 green capsicum (bell pepper), diced
    1 red capsicum (bell pepper), diced
    2 carrots, peeled and thickly sliced
    1 zucchini, thickly sliced
    2 potatoes, peeled and thickly sliced
    4 shiitake mushrooms, quartered
    2 tomatoes, quartered
    handful of coriander leaves (cilantro),
        chopped
    1 red chilli, sliced lengthways (optional)
    salt
    Couscous*

Method

1. Heat the butter and sauté the onions
    and garlic until soft. Add the chicken,
    paprika, fennel and turmeric and
    continue to sauté until fragrant.
2. Pour in the water and add the pepper
    and chickpeas. Add all the vegetables,
    the coriander leaves (cilantro) and
    the chilli (optional). Season with salt.
    Simmer for 15 minutes.
3. Serve with Couscous.

*COUSCOUS

Ingredients

    400 grams/$13^1/_2$ ounces/2 cups wheat
        couscous
    salt
    1 teaspoon butter

Method

1. Wash the couscous and soak it in water
    for 30 minutes before placing it in a
    steamer.
2. Steam for about 30 minutes and season
    with salt.
3. Just before serving, mix in the butter.

Opposite: Chicken Couscous.

SAMBAL GORENG HATI AYAM
(Spicy Chicken Liver)

Ingredients

3 tablespoons cooking oil

1 onion, peeled and sliced

6 shallots, peeled and sliced

2 cloves garlic, peeled and sliced

2 tablespoons chilli paste

4–5 stalks lemon grass, pounded

1 cm/^{1}/$_2$ inch galangal, peeled and pounded

300 grams/10^1/$_2$ ounces large prawns
(shrimps), shelled and deveined

8 chicken livers

300 grams/10^1/$_2$ ounces long beans,
diagonally sliced

4 pieces bean curd, each cut into 9 pieces
and deep-fried

4 pieces *tempe*, each cut into 6 pieces
and deep-fried

4 red chillies, sliced

4 green chillies, sliced

125 ml/4 fl oz/^{1}/$_2$ cup coconut milk,
extracted from ^{1}/$_2$ grated coconut and
125 ml/4 fl oz/^{1}/$_2$ cup water

60 ml/2 fl oz/^{1}/$_4$ cup tamarind juice,
extracted from 3 tablespoons tamarind
pulp and 60 ml/2 fl oz/
^{1}/$_4$ cup water

90 grams/3 ounces/2 cups glass noodles,
soaked in water and drained

salt

sugar

Method

1. Heat the oil and sauté the onion, shallots
    and garlic until soft. Add the chilli paste,
    lemon grass and galangal and continue
    to sauté until fragrant.

2. Stir in the prawns (shrimps) and livers,
    then add the long beans, bean curd and
    tempe. Add the red and green chillies.

3. Pour in the coconut milk and tamarind
    juice and add the glass noodles. Simmer
    for 2–3 minutes until cooked. Season
    with salt and sugar.

KUNG PAO CHICKEN

Ingredients

4 chicken breasts, cut into large cubes

2 tablespoons oyster sauce

1 teaspoon cornflour (cornstarch)

90 ml/3 fl oz/^{3}/$_8$ cup cooking oil

8 dried chillies, halved

4 cloves garlic, peeled and finely chopped

2 celery stalks, diced

1 red capsicum (bell pepper), diced

55 grams/2 ounces/^{1}/$_2$ cup canned
bamboo shoots, diced

2 teaspoons cornflour (cornstarch),
mixed with 1 tablespoon water

55 grams/2 ounces/^{1}/$_2$ cup walnuts,
lightly roasted

Sauce (blended)

60 ml/2 fl oz/^{1}/$_4$ cup balsamic vinegar

60 ml/2 fl oz/^{1}/$_4$ cup chicken stock

3 tablespoons sherry or rice wine (optional)

2 tablespoons *hoisin* sauce

1 tablespoon dark soy sauce

1 teaspoon sesame oil

2 tablespoons spicy garlic sauce

sugar

Method

1. Marinate the chicken in oyster sauce
    and cornflour (cornstarch) for
    15 minutes.

2. Heat 3 tablespoons oil and fry the
    dried chillies for 1 minute. Add the
    marinated chicken and fry for
    2 minutes. Drain.

3. In a clean pan, heat the remaining oil
    and sauté the garlic, celery, capsicum
    (bell pepper) and bamboo shoots for
    2 minutes.

4. Add the fried chicken and chillies
    together with the sauce ingredients
    and bring to a boil.

5. Add the cornflour (cornstarch)
    mixture and simmer until the sauce
    thickens. Stir in the walnuts. Serve
    immediately.

TEXAN BBQ DRUMSTICKS

Ingredients

12 chicken drumsticks

Marinade (blended)

500 ml/16 fl oz/2 cups tomato ketchup

375 ml/12 fl oz/1^1/$_2$ cups cider vinegar

250 ml/8 fl oz/1 cup olive oil

90 ml/3 fl oz/^{3}/$_8$ cup Worcestershire sauce

2 tablespoons brown sugar

1 tablespoon peeled, chopped shallots

salt

1 tablespoon Tabasco sauce

1 teaspoon cayenne pepper

125 ml/4 fl oz/^{1}/$_2$ cup water

Method

1. Combine the drumsticks with the
    marinade. Cover and refrigerate
    overnight.

2. Bring the drumsticks to room
    temperature. Remove the drumsticks
    from the marinade and set aside.

3. Simmer the marinade in a saucepan
    over medium heat until it becomes
    syrupy.

4. Grill the drumsticks on a charcoal
    grill, periodically turning them and
    basting with marinade.

5. Serve with green salad and cherry
    tomatoes.

Opposite: Texan BBQ Drumsticks.

KERUTUP AYAM KAMPUNG
(Kampung-Style Chicken Curry)

Ingredients

1 (1.5 kilograms/3 pounds, 4¹/₂ ounces)
  chicken, cut into 12 pieces

cooking oil for deep-frying

2 tablespoons dried chilli paste

2 tablespoons powdered coriander

1 tablespoon powdered fennel

1 tablespoon powdered cumin

1.5 cm/³/₄ inch cinnamon stick

3 cardamoms

750 ml/1¹/₅ pints/3 cups coconut milk,
  extracted from 1 grated coconut and
  750 ml/1¹/₅ pints/3 cups water

2 tablespoons grated palm sugar or
  brown sugar

110 grams/4 ounces/1 cup *kerisik*
  (pounded roasted grated or
  desiccated coconut)

3 pieces *asam gelugur*

salt

sugar

Marinade (finely pounded)

15 shallots, peeled

3 cloves garlic, peeled

2.5 cm/1 inch ginger, peeled

2 cm/1 inch galangal, peeled

2 stalks lemon grass, finely sliced

Method

1. Combine the chicken with the
   marinade and refrigerate for 2 hours.

2. Heat the oil and deep-fry the chicken
   until golden brown. Drain.

3. Reserve 60 ml/2 fl oz/¹/₄ cup oil and
   discard the rest. In the reserved oil,
   fry the chilli paste, coriander, fennel,
   cumin, cinnamon and cardamoms until
   fragrant.

4. Stir in the coconut milk and fried
   chicken and simmer for 20 minutes.
   Add the palm sugar or brown sugar,
   kerisik and *asam gelugur* and simmer for
   another 5 minutes. Season with salt
   and sugar.

PEPES AYAM
(Chicken Wrapped in Banana Leaf)

Ingredients

1 (1.5 kilograms/3 pounds, 4¹/₂ ounces)
  chicken, cut into 12 pieces

1 tablespoon lime juice

salt

1 tablespoon tamarind juice, extracted
  from 2 teaspoons tamarind pulp and
  1 tablespoon water

4 spring onions (scallions), cut into
  2.5-cm/1-inch lengths

5 sprigs basil (*selasih*) leaves

4 *salam* leaves, shredded

2 stalks lemon grass, bruised, cut into
  2.5-cm/1-inch lengths and shredded

1 red chilli, finely sliced

2.5 cm/1 inch galangal, peeled and
  finely sliced

banana leaves

Finely Ground Paste

2.5 cm/1 inch fresh turmeric, peeled

5 shallots, peeled

3 cloves garlic, peeled

1 tablespoon grated palm sugar
  or brown sugar

1.5 cm/³/₄ inch ginger, peeled

55 grams/2 ounces candlenuts

Method

1. Rub the chicken with lime juice and
   salt. Add the finely ground paste and
   mix well.

2. Add the tamarind juice, spring onions
   (scallions), basil leaves, *salam* leaves,
   lemon grass, chilli and galangal. Mix
   thoroughly.

3. Place 2 or 3 pieces of chicken on
   a piece of banana leaf and wrap to
   enclose. Repeat with the rest of the
   chicken.

4. Steam over boiling water for
   40 minutes.

Opposite: Pepes Ayam (Chicken Wrapped in Banana Leaf).

SAMBAL GORENG AYAM EMAK
(Mother's Chicken Sambal)

Ingredients

- 12 pieces chicken
- 1 tablespoon powdered turmeric
- 1 teaspoon salt
- cooking oil for deep-frying
- 3 sprigs curry leaves
- 60 ml/2 fl oz/$^1/_4$ cup tamarind juice, extracted from 1 tablespoon tamarind pulp and 60 ml/2 fl oz/$^1/_4$ cup water
- 60 ml/2 fl oz/$^1/_4$ cup water
- 3 potatoes, peeled, cut into wedges and deep-fried
- 2 tomatoes, quartered
- salt
- sugar

Finely Ground Paste

- 20 dried chillies, seeded, soaked in water and drained
- 1$^1/_2$ tablespoons coriander seeds
- 1 tablespoon fennel seeds
- 1 tablespoon cumin seeds
- 1 cm/$^1/_2$ inch ginger, peeled
- 4 cloves garlic, peeled
- 8 shallots, peeled

Method

1. Rub the chicken with turmeric and salt.
2. Heat the oil and deep-fry the chicken just until cooked. Do not let it become crisp. Drain.
3. Reserve 3 tablespoons oil and discard the rest. In the reserved oil, sauté the finely ground paste together with the curry leaves until fragrant.
4. Add the fried chicken, tamarind juice and water. Cook until the gravy is thick, then add the potatoes and tomatoes. Season with salt and sugar and stir for 2 minutes.

STEAMED GINGER CHICKEN

Ingredients

- 1 large round or square piece of soft bean curd
- 140 grams/5 ounces boneless chicken, diced
- 2 tablespoons cooking oil
- 2 shallots, peeled and sliced
- 1 clove garlic, peeled and finely chopped
- 2 black Chinese mushrooms, soaked in water and diced
- 3 water chestnuts, peeled and diced
- 2 cm/1 inch young ginger, peeled and finely sliced
- 1 teaspoon cornflour (cornstarch), mixed with 1 tablespoon water
- 1 spring onion (scallion), chopped
- 1 red chilli, seeded and chopped

Bean Curd Marinade (blended)

- $^1/_4$ teaspoon salt
- $^1/_4$ teaspoon ground white pepper
- $^1/_4$ teaspoon sugar
- $^1/_2$ tablespoon vegetable oil

Chicken Marinade (mixed)

- $^1/_4$ teaspoon salt
- $^1/_4$ teaspoon ground white pepper
- $^1/_4$ teaspoon sugar
- $^1/_2$ teaspoon cornflour (cornstarch)

Sauce (blended)

- 180 ml/6 fl oz/$^3/_4$ cup water
- 1 teaspoon chicken stock granules
- 2 teaspoons light soy sauce
- 1 teaspoon oyster sauce
- $^1/_2$ teaspoon sugar
- $^1/_4$ teaspoon ground black pepper

Method

1. Marinate the bean curd and chicken in their respective marinades for 15 minutes.
2. Place the bean curd in a heatproof dish and steam over rapidly boiling water for 10 minutes. Set aside.
3. Heat the oil and lightly brown the shallots and garlic. Add the mushrooms and stir-fry for 1 minute. Add the marinated chicken and toss until the meat changes colour. Add the water chestnuts and young ginger and stir-fry for 30 seconds. Pour in the sauce ingredients and bring the mixture to a boil.
4. Simmer for 2 minutes. Thicken with the cornflour (cornstarch) mixture and stir in the spring onion (scallion) and chilli.
5. Pour over the steamed bean curd.

Opposite: Sambal Goreng Ayam Emak (Mother's Chicken Sambal).

120
Portuguese Baked Fish
Ikan Percik
(Grilled Fish)
Pepes Ikan Kembung
(Spicy Chubb Mackerel Paste
in Banana Leaf)

122
Hor Mok
(Thai Steamed Fish Mousse)
Tod Mun Pla
(Thai Fish Cakes)
Kemaaina Tangy
Grilled Snapper

124
Otak-otak Makanan Laut
(Seafood Otak-otak in Coconut)
Ikan Bakar Rica-rica
(Rica-rica Grilled Fish)
Pla Sam Rod
(Thai Fried Fish with Chillies)

126
Fish and Chips
Ikan Pesmol
(Fish in Spicy Coconut Milk Gravy)
Ikan Kurau Berkuah Tauco
(Fish in Preserved Soy Beans)

128
Steamed Fish
Jelawat Masak Tom Yam
(Jelawat in Tom Yam Gravy)
Ikan Kukus Berempah
(Spicy Steamed Fish)

130
Chilli Crab
Caldeirada de Peixe
(Portuguese Fish Stew)
Ikan Sembilang Lemak
Cili Api Jandaku
(My Ex-Wife's Catfish in
Bird's Eye Chilli Gravy)

132
Nyonya-Style Fried Squid
Ikan Santan Berlada
(Fish in Spicy Coconut Gravy)
Siakap Asam Tumis
(Sea Bass in Tangy Gravy)

134
Thai Pineapple Prawn (Shrimp)
Curry
Crab Balls with Mango Sauce

136
Kerala Coconut Prawns (Shrimps)
Ketam Goreng Istimewa
(Special Fried Chilli Crab)
Spicy Tom Yam Fried Crab

138
Snapper Fillet Piccatta
Stir-Fried Prawns (Shrimps)
with Pineapple
Saffron Squid with Tomato

140
Masala Prawns (Shrimps)
Lala Tumis Pedas
(Chilli Fried Clams)
Selada Udang Rampai
(Hot and Tangy Prawns [Shrimps])

142
Sambal Sotong Kering Emak
(Mother's Dried Squid in Chilli Sauce)
Kenus Mebase
(Squid Curry)
Thai Pineapple Seafood
Curry

144
Rendang Kerang
(Cockle Rendang)
Kalio Udang Tempoyak
(Prawns [Shrimps] in Preserved Durian
Gravy)
Rendang Udang Harimau
(Tiger Prawn Rendang)

S
E
A
F
O
O
D

I must confess that fishing has never been a great passion with me, as it seems to require more patience than I normally have. When I was eight years old, my father often took me along when he went fishing at an unused mining pool near our home. I hated sitting next to him just waiting for the next catch. All I could think about was being home with my two sisters playing *masak-masak* (play cooking)! My father used to whisper in my ear, *"Orang laki-laki mesti pandai pancing ikan, barulah orang perempuan boleh masak!* (Men must know how to fish; only then will women be able to cook!)." But I never heeded his advice. I remember telling my father, when I was eleven, that I hated fishing. But cooking and eating fish … well, that's a different story.

Seafood seems to be everyone's favourite these days, for health or other reasons. Both my kids jump off their feet the minute I suggest going out to dinner at a seafood restaurant.

The key to producing a fabulous seafood meal is knowing how to choose the ingredients. Get acquainted with your fishmongers. Establish a good relationship with them to develop trust and create a situation of accountability in getting the freshest seafood from them.

Fresh fish has a faint, clean scent of the sea. Never buy seafood that has a strong fishy odour. Top-quality seafood—the only kind you want to eat—should be bright and sparkling clean. It is easy to recognise it once you know how to use two simple tools. The first is your nose. Take a sniff. Any odour is an instant sign of decay. The second tool is your eyes. I always look first at the fish counter and then at the fish. The counter should be clean, and the seafood should be nicely swaddled in ice. The eyes and skin of the fish should be shiny and bright, the scales should be tight against the skin, and the gills should be clear red. You may have to pull back the covering flap to check on this. The flesh should be firm to the touch, springing back when it is pressed. If the eyes are sunken, or if the fish looks dull, is soft to the touch or has a strong fishy odour, don't buy it! You will not be able to make it taste good. Never mind all the advice from older people who say that it can be washed with lime juice or even with a mixture of plain (all-purpose) flour and water. It doesn't work. Just feed the cat!

Seafood is perishable and should be consumed as quickly as possible. Do not keep any fish for more than two days in the refrigerator without freezing it. When you bring it home, rinse it thoroughly under cold water and pat it dry with paper towels. Cover it loosely with wax paper so that the air can circulate around it, and store it in the coldest part of the refrigerator, preferably on a bed of ice. Fresh crabs and prawns (shrimps) can be frozen, but the taste and texture will not be the same. Hard-shell seafood, such as oysters, clams and mussels, cannot be frozen but will keep for several days in the refrigerator. The water should be poured off as it accumulates.

SEAFOOD

Temperature is the key to maintaining food quality. Spoilage occurs twice as fast at 4°C/40°F, the usual temperature of a home refrigerator, than at 0°C/32°F, which is the ideal storage temperature. A whole fish keeps longer if it has been gutted. This eliminates the enzymes in the stomach that accelerate decay. A fish that has been cut into pieces or fillets deteriorates more rapidly than a whole fish, because exposed flesh is more vulnerable to bacteria. For this reason, it is best to buy fish at a market that cuts it on the spot rather than retailing it pre-cut. Alternatively, you could purchase a whole fish and cut it yourself.

If seafood is frozen, it is best to thaw it slowly in the refrigerator before cooking, to maintain its texture and minimise moisture loss. One thing you should never do, unless you are in a hurry, is soak it in water to speed up the thawing process. That will destroy the taste as well as the texture.

Many cooking methods are appropriate for fish and shellfish. Grilling is one of my favourites for its ease, the delicate taste it imparts and its sheer simplicity, to say nothing of the natural exhaust system outdoors. Broiling is always an alternative to grilling, though it doesn't impart quite the same flavour to the fish. Other methods are poaching, baking, sautéing and steaming, all of which yield fine results.

Fish cooks quickly, because its flesh is extremely tender and delicate. Care must always be taken to cook it just to the point of juicy perfection, otherwise it can taste dry and insipid. There are several ways to determine when fish is sufficiently cooked. The rule of thumb for estimating the required cooking time is 10 minutes per inch of thickness for fresh fish. The rule can be applied to baking, broiling, grilling, braising, pan-frying or deep-frying. This produces fish that flakes easily when gently probed with a knife or fork, which is equivalent to cooking meat to the medium well or well-done stage.

A very simple but less exacting test is to insert the tip of a small, sharp paring knife into the thickest part of a fish fillet or steak during the cooking. Leave the knife tip in the fish for approximately 5 seconds, then withdraw it and carefully test by feeling the knife tip with your finger or the sensitive centre of your lower lip. When the knife feels hot to the touch, the fish is cooked. (I prefer not to do this test!) Another way to gauge doneness (this takes considerable experience) is to gently press the fish at its thickest point. When it feels springy as opposed to slack, it is sufficiently cooked.

Going to the fish market always inspires me with new ideas. A perfect piece of fish really makes me eager to see what I can do with it. While working in Hawaii many years ago, I prepared fish in all sorts of elaborate ways. But now I favour simpler methods.

After going through the following wonderful seafood recipes, I hope you will be ready to dash out of the door with your rod and start fishing as a hobby or just end up having fun at the market, like me. Good luck, and remember to put your bait!

PORTUGUESE BAKED FISH

Ingredients

- 60 ml/2 fl oz/¼ cup cooking oil
- juice of ½ lime
- ½ tablespoon dark soy sauce
- salt
- sugar
- 1 (600 grams/1 pounds, 5 ounces) pomfret
- banana leaf

Finely Pounded Paste

- 4 red chillies
- 4 candlenuts
- 8 shallots, peeled
- 1 stalk lemon grass, finely sliced
- ½ teaspoon shrimp paste
- 1 tablespoon powdered chilli
- 2 kaffir lime leaves

Method

1. Heat the oil and sauté the finely pounded paste over low heat until fragrant. Add the lime juice, soy sauce, salt and sugar.
2. Spread the cooked paste over the fish and wrap the fish in a piece of banana leaf.
3. Bake in a 180°C/350°F preheated oven for 20 minutes or grill over glowing charcoal.

IKAN PERCIK
(Grilled Fish)

Ingredients

- 600 grams/1 pounds, 5 ounces grouper fillet, cut into slices about 200 grams/7 ounces each
- 3 tablespoons cooking oil
- 125 ml/4 fl oz/½ cup coconut milk, extracted from ½ grated coconut and 125 ml/4 fl oz/½ cup water
- salt

Finely Ground Paste

- 3 stalks lemon grass, finely sliced
- 10 shallots, peeled
- 4 cloves garlic, peeled
- 2 cm/1 inch ginger, peeled
- 2 cm/1 inch fresh turmeric, peeled
- 6 candlenuts
- 1 tablespoon sugar
- salt
- freshly cracked black pepper

Method

1. Mix the fish with half the finely ground paste and marinate for 1 hour.
2. Heat the oil and sauté the remaining half of the finely ground paste until fragrant.
3. Stir in the coconut milk and simmer until the sauce thickens. Add salt if necessary.
4. Grill the fish over glowing charcoal, periodically turning the slices and basting with cooked sauce.
5. Serve the fish with the remaining sauce.

PEPES IKAN KEMBUNG
(Spicy Chubb Mackerel Paste in Banana Leaf)

Ingredients

- 55 grams/2 ounces/¼ cup tom yam paste
- 60 ml/2 fl oz/¼ cup coconut milk, extracted from ½ grated coconut and 60 ml/2 fl oz/¼ cup water
- 2 teaspoons light soy sauce
- 500 grams/1 pound, 1½ ounces boned chubb mackerel
- 4 kaffir lime leaves, finely sliced
- salt
- juice of 2 limes
- 100 grams/3½ ounces cabbage leaves, blanched and drained
- banana leaves

Finely Ground Paste

- 2 onions, peeled
- 4 cloves garlic, peeled
- 2.5 cm/1 inch ginger, peeled
- 1 cm/½ inch fresh turmeric, peeled
- 2 tablespoons rice, roasted

Method

1. Mix the finely ground paste with the tom yam paste, coconut milk, soy sauce, mackerel, kaffir lime leaves, salt and lime juice.
2. Place 2 tablespoons of the mixture on a cabbage leaf, wrap and transfer to a piece of banana leaf. Fold the banana leaf and secure both ends with toothpicks.
3. Steam the pepes for 20 minutes over boiling water.

Opposite: Portuguese Baked Fish.

HOR MOK
(Thai Steamed Fish Mousse)

Ingredients

- 500 ml/16 fl oz/2 cups coconut milk, extracted from 1 grated coconut and 500 ml/16 fl oz/2 cups water
- 1 teaspoon rice flour
- 600 grams/1 pounds, 5 ounces boned Spanish mackerel, minced (ground)
- 1 egg, beaten
- 2 tablespoons *nam pla*
- 1 teaspoon sugar
- 15–20 banana leaf cups, 7.5 cm/3 inches in diameter
- 1 sprig basil (*selasih*) leaves
- 3 kaffir lime leaves, finely sliced
- 2 tablespoons chopped coriander leaves (cilantro)
- 1 red chilli, finely sliced

Curry Spices (finely ground)

- 5 dried chillies, seeded, soaked in water and drained
- 7 shallots, peeled
- 3 cloves garlic, peeled
- 2 tablespoons peeled, finely sliced galangal
- 2 tablespoons finely sliced lemon grass
- 1 tablespoon chopped coriander root
- 1 teaspoon ground white pepper
- 1 teaspoon salt
- 1 teaspoon shrimp paste

Method

1. Mix 250 ml/8 fl oz/1 cup coconut milk with the rice flour and cook over medium heat until it boils and forms a paste. Remove from heat and set aside.

2. In a large mixing bowl, combine the ground curry spices with the remaining 250 ml/8 fl oz/1 cup coconut milk, mackerel, egg, *nam pla* and sugar. Stir well.

3. Line the bottoms of the banana leaf cups with basil leaves, fill them with fish mixture and steam for 15–20 minutes.

4. Remove from heat. Pour some cooked coconut paste on each hor mok and sprinkle with kaffir lime leaves, coriander leaves (cilantro) and chilli. Steam for another minute.

TOD MUN PLA
(Thai Fish Cakes)

Ingredients

- 300 grams/10½ ounces boned Spanish mackerel, minced (ground)
- 1 tablespoon Thai red curry paste
- 1 stalk lemon grass, finely sliced
- 1 kaffir lime leaf, finely sliced
- 2 teaspoons *nam pla*
- 1 egg yolk, beaten
- 1 tablespoon cornflour (cornstarch)
- 6 long beans, finely sliced
- 4 bird's eye chillies, finely sliced
- cooking oil for pan-frying
- lettuce, torn into large pieces
- cucumber, sliced
- tomato, sliced

Method

1. Combine the mackerel with all the other ingredients except oil, lettuce, cucumber and tomato. Refrigerate for 1 hour.

2. With oiled palms, shape the mixture into slightly flattened balls.

3. Pan-fry the balls in hot oil.

4. Garnish with lettuce, cucumber and tomato.

Note: This dish can be served with cucumber pickle.

KEMAAINA TANGY GRILLED SNAPPER

The Hawaiian word *kemaaina* means 'traditional'.

Ingredients

- 1 (600 grams/1 pounds, 5 ounces) snapper
- banana leaf
- 45 grams/1½ ounces/¼ cup grated pineapple
- juice of 1 lime
- 1 red chilli, finely chopped
- 1 clove garlic, peeled and finely chopped
- 2 tablespoons dark soy sauce
- 1 tablespoon peeled, sliced young ginger
- freshly cracked black pepper
- 55 grams/2 ounces/½ cup grated coconut
- 1 sprig coriander leaves (cilantro), chopped

Method

1. Place the fish on a piece of banana leaf. Top with the pineapple, lime juice, chilli, garlic, soy sauce, ginger and pepper. Sprinkle with coconut and coriander leaves (cilantro).

2. Wrap and secure both ends of the banana leaf with toothpicks. Grill over glowing charcoal for 15–20 minutes.

Opposite: Tod Mun Pla (Thai Fish Cakes).

OTAK-OTAK MAKANAN LAUT
(Seafood Otak-otak in Coconut)

Ingredients

- 1 young coconut
- 2 tablespoons cooking oil
- 2 tablespoons Thai red curry paste
- 400 grams/14 ounces boned Spanish mackerel, finely chopped
- 300 grams/10^1/$_2$ ounces prawns (shrimps), shelled, deveined and finely chopped
- 250 ml/8 fl oz/1 cup coconut milk, extracted from ^{1}/$_2$ grated coconut and 250 ml/8 fl oz/1 cup water
- 300 grams/10^1/$_2$ ounces crabmeat
- 1 cm/^{1}/$_2$ inch galangal, peeled and finely sliced
- 3 kaffir lime leaves, finely sliced
- 1 sprig basil (*selasih*) leaves, finely sliced
- 1 tablespoon *nam pla*
- 2 teaspoons lime juice
- 1 teaspoon sugar
- 1 red chilli, finely sliced
- 2 tablespoons chopped coriander leaves (cilantro)
- 1 teaspoon cornflour (cornstarch)
- 1 tablespoon *kerisik* (pounded roasted grated or desiccated coconut)

Method

1. Cut through the top ^{1}/$_8$ of the coconut and scoop out the flesh.
2. Heat the oil and fry the Thai red curry paste until fragrant. Add the fish and prawns (shrimps) and stir well.
3. Add the remaining ingredients, including the reserved coconut flesh. Mix well and transfer into the coconut shell.
4. Bake in a 180°C/350°F preheated oven for 30 minutes until the otak-otak boils and becomes almost dry.
5. Serve immediately.

IKAN BAKAR RICA-RICA
(Rica-rica Grilled Fish)

Ingredients

- 1 (700 grams/1^1/$_2$ pound) Spanish mackerel
- juice of 6 *kalamansi*, divided into two portions
- salt
- 8 red chillies
- 10 shallots, peeled
- 1 cm/^{1}/$_2$ inch ginger, peeled
- 60 ml/2 fl oz/^{1}/$_4$ cup cooking oil

Method

1. Rub the fish with one portion of *kalamansi* juice and salt. Set aside for at least 1 hour, preferably overnight.
2. Finely pound the chillies, shallots and ginger. Add the remaining portion of *kalamansi* juice. Divide the paste into two portions.
3. Rub one portion of paste over the fish and grill the fish over glowing charcoal, turning it periodically.
4. Heat the oil and gently fry the other half of the paste until fragrant. Season with salt. Serve along with the grilled fish.

Note: In North Sulawesi, the fish commonly used in this dish is tuna.

PLA SAM ROD
(Thai Fried Fish with Chillies)

Ingredients

- 1 (1 kilogram/2 pounds, 3 ounces) sea bass
- 30 grams/1 ounce/^{1}/$_4$ cup cornflour (cornstarch)
- ^{1}/$_2$ teaspoon salt
- ^{1}/$_2$ teaspoon sugar
- 1 egg yolk, beaten
- cooking oil for shallow-frying
- Hot and Sour Sauce*
- 3 kaffir lime leaves, finely sliced

Method

1. Combine the fish with the cornflour (cornstarch), salt, sugar and egg yolk and shallow-fry in hot oil until crisp. Drain and place on a serving dish. Reserve 60 ml/2 fl oz/^{1}/$_4$ cup oil and discard the rest.
2. Pour Hot and Sour Sauce over the fish and garnish with kaffir lime leaves.

*HOT AND SOUR SAUCE

Ingredients

- 8 red chillies, finely pounded
- 2 cloves garlic, peeled and finely pounded
- 2 tablespoons coriander leaves (cilantro), chopped
- 60 ml/2 fl oz/^{1}/$_4$ cup tamarind juice, extracted from 1 tablespoon tamarind pulp and 60 ml/2 fl oz/^{1}/$_4$ cup water
- 1 teaspoon vinegar
- 3 tablespoons sugar
- 1 tablespoon *nam pla*

Method

1. In the reserved oil, sauté the chillies, garlic and coriander leaves (cilantro) until fragrant.
2. Add the tamarind juice, vinegar, sugar and *nam pla*. Stir well and bring to a boil.

Opposite: Otak-otak Makanan Laut (Seafood Otak-otak in Coconut).

FISH AND CHIPS

Ingredients

- 4 thick fillets of any white boneless fish, e.g., threadfin, cod, snapper
- salt
- freshly cracked black pepper
- Batter*
- cooking oil for deep-frying
- lemon, cut into wedges
- potato chips
- tartar sauce or tomato ketchup

Method

1. Season the fish with salt and pepper.
2. Heat the oil to 160°C/325°F. Dip the fish fillets into batter and fry, 2 pieces at a time, for 7–8 minutes until crisp and deep golden brown. Drain and arrange on a serving dish.
3. Serve with lemon wedges, potato chips and tartar sauce or tomato ketchup.

*BATTER

Ingredients

- 15 grams/¹/₂ ounce fresh yeast
- 310 ml/10¹/₂ fl oz/1¹/₄ cups beer
- 225 grams/8 ounces/1 cup plain (all-purpose) flour
- 1 teaspoon salt
- ¹/₂ teaspoon ground white pepper

Method

1. Cream the yeast with a little beer to make a smooth paste. Gradually stir in the rest of the beer.
2. Sift the flour, salt and pepper into a bowl. Make a well in the centre and pour in the beer mixture. Slowly incorporate the liquid into the flour to make a smooth batter. Cover and leave at room temperature for 1 hour.

IKAN PESMOL
(Fish in Spicy Coconut Milk Gravy)

Ingredients

- 1 (1 kilogram/2 pounds, 3 ounces) sea bass
- salt
- freshly cracked black pepper
- cooking oil for shallow-frying + 3 tablespoons
- 1 stalk lemon grass, bruised
- 2 cm/1 inch galangal, peeled and bruised
- 10 bird's eye chillies
- 2 kaffir lime leaves
- 2 *salam* leaves
- 500 ml/16 fl oz/2 cups coconut milk, extracted from 1 grated coconut and 500 ml/16 fl oz/2 cups water
- juice of 1 lime
- sugar

Finely Ground Paste

- 5 red chillies
- 10 bird's eye chillies
- 4 shallots, peeled
- 2 cloves garlic, peeled
- 10 candlenuts
- ¹/₂ teaspoon powdered turmeric
- 2.5 cm/1 inch ginger, peeled

Method

1. Rub the fish with salt and pepper and shallow-fry in hot oil until crisp and golden brown. Drain and place on a serving dish.
2. Heat 3 tablespoons oil and sauté the finely ground paste until fragrant. Add the lemon grass and galangal. Add the chillies, kaffir lime leaves and *salam* leaves. Pour in the coconut milk and simmer until the gravy thickens. Season with lime juice, salt and sugar.
3. Pour the gravy over the fried fish and serve immediately.

IKAN KURAU BERKUAH TAUCO
(Fish in Preserved Soy Beans)

Ingredients

- 3 large pieces threadfin
- salt
- freshly cracked black pepper
- cooking oil for shallow-frying + 60 ml/ 2 fl oz/¹/₄ cup
- 3 cloves garlic, peeled and finely chopped
- 1 cm/¹/₂ inch ginger, peeled and sliced
- 3 tomatoes, cut into small cubes
- 2 tablespoons *tau cheo* (preserved soy beans), washed under running water
- 3 spring onions (scallions), chopped

Sauce (blended)

- 2 teaspoons oyster sauce
- ¹/₄ teaspoon sugar
- 1 teaspoon sesame oil
- pinch of salt
- 2 tablespoons cornflour (cornstarch)
- 60 ml/2 fl oz/¹/₄ cup chicken stock

Method

1. Rub the fish with salt and pepper and shallow-fry in hot oil until crisp. Drain and set aside.
2. In a clean wok, heat 60 ml/2 fl oz/ ¹/₄ cup oil and sauté the garlic and ginger.
3. Add the tomatoes and *tau cheo* and cook until the tomatoes are soft. Add the sauce ingredients and bring to a simmer.
4. Add the spring onions (scallions) and fish and stir until the sauce is cooked.

Opposite: Ikan Pesmol (Fish in Coconut Milk Gravy).

STEAMED FISH

Ingredients

1 (500 grams/1 pound, 1¹/₂ ounces)
   snapper or sea bass
2 teaspoons *nam pla*
¹/₂ teaspoon cornflour (cornstarch)
coriander leaves (cilantro), chopped
spring onion (scallion), sliced

Finely Sliced

1 torch ginger bud
1 stalk lemon grass
5 red chillies
2 kaffir lime leaves
1 cm/¹/₂ inch young ginger, peeled
2 cloves garlic, peeled
1 sprig coriander leaves (cilantro)
1 spring onion (scallion)

Seasoning

salt
1¹/₂ tablespoons sugar
3–3¹/₂ tablespoons *kalamansi* juice
¹/₂ teaspoon anchovy stock granules
³/₄ teaspoon cornflour (cornstarch)

Method

1. Marinate the fish in the *nam pla* and cornflour (cornstarch) for 10 minutes. Place it on a greased serving dish.

2. Combine the finely sliced ingredients and the seasoning. Pour over the fish and steam over rapidly boiling water for 5 minutes.

3. Garnish with coriander leaves (cilantro) and spring onion (scallion) and serve immediately.

JELAWAT MASAK TOM YAM
(Jelawat in Tom Yam Gravy)

Jelawat (*Leptobarbus hoeveni*) is a freshwater fish popular with Malaysians.

Ingredients

90 ml/3 fl oz/³/₈ cup cooking oil
2 eggplants, quartered
4 lady's fingers (okra), stemmed
2 tablespoons tom yam paste
125 ml/4 fl oz/¹/₂ cup water
125 ml/4 fl oz/¹/₂ cup coconut milk,
   extracted from ¹/₂ grated coconut
   and 125 ml/4 fl oz/¹/₂ cup water
1 tomato, halved
5 bird's eye chillies
1 torch ginger bud, halved lengthways
1 (500 grams/1 pound, 1¹/₂ ounces)
   jelawat
juice of 1 lime
2 kaffir lime leaves, finely sliced

Method

1. Heat 60 ml/2 fl oz/¹/₄ cup oil and stir-fry the eggplants and lady's fingers (okra). Drain and set aside.

2. In a clean wok, heat the remaining oil and sauté the tom yam paste until fragrant. Pour in the water and coconut milk and bring to a simmer.

3. Add the fried eggplants and lady's fingers (okra), tomato, chillies and torch ginger bud. Simmer for 5 minutes.

4. Add the fish and simmer for 10 minutes before adding the lime juice.

5. Just before serving, garnish with kaffir lime leaves.

IKAN KUKUS BEREMPAH
(Spicy Steamed Fish)

Ingredients

1 spring onion (scallion), chopped
1 (600 grams/1 pounds, 5 ounces)
   sea bass
lemon or lime, sliced
cucumber, sliced

Finely Ground Paste

20 bird's eye chillies
1 torch ginger bud, finely sliced
3 stalks lemon grass, finely sliced
3 kaffir lime leaves

Seasoning (blended)

3 tablespoons cooking oil
3 tablespoons lime juice
1 tablespoon *nam pla*
1 tablespoon sugar

Method

1. Arrange the spring onion (scallion) in a heatproof dish. Top with the fish.

2. Combine the finely ground paste with the seasoning and pour over the fish.

3. Steam over rapidly boiling water for 5 minutes.

4. Garnish with lemon or lime and cucumber. Serve hot.

Opposite: Steamed Fish.

CHILLI CRAB

Ingredients

cooking oil for deep-frying + 2 tablespoons

1.2–1.5 kilograms/2 pounds, 10 ounces–
   3 pounds, 4¹/₂ ounces crabs, halved

2 tablespoons cornflour (cornstarch),
   mixed with 60 ml/2 fl oz/¹/₄ cup
   water

1 egg, beaten

spring onion (scallion), chopped

Finely Ground Paste

1¹/₂ tablespoons powdered chilli

6 red chillies

6 cloves garlic, peeled

100 grams/3¹/₂ ounces shallots, peeled

1 cm/¹/₂ inch ginger, peeled

Sauce (blended)

3 tablespoons chilli sauce

2 tablespoons sugar

2 tablespoons vinegar

250 ml/8 fl oz/1 cup canned
   tomato sauce

salt

Method

1. Heat the oil and deep-fry the crabs
   until golden. Drain and set aside.

2. Heat 2 tablespoons oil and sauté the
   finely ground paste until fragrant. Stir
   in the sauce ingredients and bring the
   mixture to a boil.

3. Cover and simmer for about
   10 minutes.

4. Gradually add the cornflour
   (cornstarch) mixture and stir well.
   Add the beaten egg. Gently stir in the
   fried crabs and simmer until the sauce
   is cooked.

5. Garnish with spring onion (scallion)
   and serve immediately.

CALDEIRADA DE PEIXE
(Portuguese Fish Stew)

Most coastal regions of Portugal have
their own varieties of fish stew. This is my
favourite. The stock is made of fish bones,
heads and trimmings. Normally the soup
is puréed before being served, but I think
it looks more attractive left as it is.

Ingredients

90 ml/3 fl oz/³/₈ cup olive oil

1 onion, peeled and chopped

5 cloves garlic, peeled and minced

3 celery stalks, chopped

2 leeks, chopped

1 can (411 grams/14¹/₂ ounces) Italian
   plum tomatoes, mashed

1 tablespoon tomato purée (tomato paste)

¹/₂ red capsicum (bell pepper), finely diced

1 fresh bay leaf

5 cm/2 inch strip orange rind

500 ml/16 fl oz/2 cups fish stock

300 grams/10¹/₂ ounces mixed fish—
   snapper, mackerel, etc.—diced

salt

pinch of cayenne pepper

freshly cracked black pepper

fresh parsley, chopped

Method

1. Heat the oil and sauté the onion,
   garlic, celery and leeks for 5 minutes.

2. Add the tomatoes, tomato purée
   (tomato paste), capsicum (bell
   pepper), bay leaf and orange rind.
   Cook for 5 minutes.

3. Add the fish stock and bring to a
   simmer. Add the fish and simmer for
   5 minutes. Season with salt, cayenne
   pepper and black pepper.

4. Just before serving, garnish
   with parsley.

IKAN SEMBILANG LEMAK CILI API JANDAKU
(My Ex-Wife's Catfish in Bird's Eye Chilli Gravy)

My ex-wife makes the best lemak cili api
(Catfish in Bird's Eye Chilli Gravy) that I
have ever tasted. Over the years I have not
been able to acquire her skills, despite my
vast culinary knowledge. Although people
who come from Negeri Sembilan swear
that their recipe is the best, my ex-wife
says that she is from Malacca and her
recipe is better! So test it out. This dish
must be cooked in a *belanga* (clay pot).

Ingredients

8 *ikan sembilang* (catfish), cleaned and
   barbecued over glowing charcoal

juice of 3 limes

750 ml/1¹/₅ pints/3 cups second-squeeze
   coconut milk and 500 ml/16 fl oz/
   2 cups first-squeeze coconut milk,
   extracted from 1¹/₂ grated coconuts

salt

Finely Pounded Paste

30 bird's eye chillies

2 cm/1 inch fresh turmeric, peeled

Method

1. In a *belanga* (clay pot), combine the
   ikan sembilang with the lime juice and
   finely pounded paste. Cook over low
   heat for 10 minutes to shrink the fish.

2. Add the second-squeeze coconut milk
   and simmer for 10 minutes.

3. Add the first-squeeze coconut milk
   and simmer for 5 minutes.

4. Season with salt and more lime juice
   if necessary.

Opposite: Chilli Crab.

NYONYA-STYLE FRIED SQUID

Ingredients

5 tablespoons cooking oil
500 grams/1 pound, 1 1/2 ounces squid, cut lengthways and scored diagonally
salt
sugar
juice of 1/2 lime
handful of mint leaves, chopped
1 teaspoon cornflour (cornstarch), mixed with 1 tablespoon water

Finely Ground Paste

5 red chillies
10 shallots, peeled
4 cloves garlic, peeled
1 cm/1/2 inch ginger, peeled
1 cm/1/2 inch fresh turmeric, peeled
2 stalks lemon grass, finely sliced
1 torch ginger bud, finely sliced
1 tablespoon shrimp paste

Sauce (blended)

2 tablespoons canned tomato sauce
2 tablespoons chilli sauce
1 tablespoon light soy sauce
1 teaspoon sugar

Method

1. Heat the oil and sauté the finely ground paste until fragrant.
2. Add the squid, sauce ingredients, salt and sugar and cook for 2 minutes.
3. Add the lime juice and mint leaves. Pour in the cornflour (cornstarch) mixture and cook until the sauce thickens.

IKAN SANTAN BERLADA
(Fish in Spicy Coconut Gravy)

Ingredients

1 (1 kilogram/2 pounds, 3 ounces) threadfin
salt
freshly cracked black pepper
1 tablespoon cornflour (cornstarch)
cooking oil for deep-frying + 60 ml/ 2 fl oz/1/4 cup
500 ml/16 fl oz/2 cups coconut milk, extracted from 1 grated coconut and 500 ml/16 fl oz/2 cups water
60 ml/2 fl oz/1/4 cup tamarind juice, extracted from 1 1/2 tablespoons tamarind pulp and 60 ml/2 fl oz/ 1/4 cup water
sugar

Finely Ground Paste

12 dried chillies, seeded, soaked in water and drained
2 teaspoons shrimp paste
3 tablespoons coriander seeds, roasted
1 tablespoon cumin seeds, roasted
1/2 tablespoon fennel seeds, roasted
2 onions, peeled
6 cloves garlic, peeled
1 stalk lemon grass, finely sliced
1.5 cm/3/4 inch ginger, peeled
2.5 cm/1 inch galangal, peeled

Whole Spices

3 cloves
3 cardamoms
2 cm/1 inch cinnamon stick

Method

1. Rub the fish with salt and pepper. Rub with cornflour (cornstarch) and deep-fry in hot oil until crisp. Drain and place on a serving dish.
2. Heat 60 ml/2 fl oz/1/4 cup oil and sauté the finely ground paste until fragrant. Add the whole spices.
3. Stir in the coconut milk, tamarind juice, salt and sugar. Simmer until the gravy thickens.
4. Pour the gravy over the fish and serve immediately.

SIAKAP ASAM TUMIS
(Sea Bass in Tangy Gravy)

Ingredients

60 ml/2 fl oz/1/4 cup vegetable oil
125 ml/4 fl oz/1/2 cup tamarind juice, extracted from 1 tablespoon tamarind pulp and 125 ml/4 fl oz/1/2 cup water
250 ml/8 fl oz/1 cup water
6 lady's fingers (okra), stemmed
1 large *siakap* (sea bass), cut into 4 pieces
1 bunch *kesum* leaves
salt
sugar

Finely Ground Paste

4 tablespoons chilli paste
1 tablespoon shrimp paste
6 shallots, peeled
1 cm/1/2 inch fresh turmeric, peeled
3 cloves garlic, peeled
1 kaffir lime leaf

Method

1. Heat the oil and sauté the finely ground paste until fragrant. Add the tamarind juice, water and lady's fingers (okra) and simmer for 10 minutes.
2. Add the fish and *kesum* leaves. Simmer for another 5 minutes. Season with salt and sugar.

Opposite: Nyonya-Style Fried Squid.

THAI PINEAPPLE PRAWN (SHRIMP) CURRY

Ingredients

- 3 tablespoons cooking oil
- 500 ml/16 fl oz/2 cups coconut milk, extracted from 1 grated coconut and 500 ml/16 fl oz/2 cups water
- 3 kaffir lime leaves
- 2 tablespoons *nam pla*
- salt
- sugar
- 350 grams/12 ounces/2 cups sliced pineapple
- 700 grams/1$\frac{1}{2}$ pound medium freshwater prawns (shrimps), legs and feelers removed
- handful of basil (*selasih*) leaves

Finely Ground Paste

- 10 red chillies
- 2 stalks lemon grass, finely sliced
- 1 cm/$\frac{1}{2}$ inch galangal, peeled
- 3 sprigs coriander leaves (cilantro)
- 2 teaspoons chopped kaffir lime leaves
- 10 black peppercorns
- 2 teaspoons powdered cumin
- 1 teaspoon shrimp paste
- 2 teaspoons powdered turmeric

Method

1. Heat the oil and sauté the finely ground paste until fragrant.
2. Stir in the coconut milk, kaffir lime leaves, *nam pla*, salt, sugar and pineapple. Simmer until the oil starts separating.
3. Add the prawns (shrimps) and basil leaves and simmer for 3 minutes.

CRAB BALLS WITH MANGO SAUCE

Ingredients

- 300 grams/10$\frac{1}{2}$ ounces crabmeat
- 1 medium potato, boiled, peeled and mashed
- 2 slices bread, soaked in 2 tablespoons milk and mashed
- 1 red chilli, finely chopped
- 60 ml/2 fl oz/$\frac{1}{4}$ cup mayonnaise
- 2 teaspoons tom yam paste
- 1 kaffir lime leaf or handful of *kesum* leaves, sliced
- salt
- 110 grams/4 ounces/1 cup breadcrumbs
- 85 grams/3 ounces/$\frac{1}{2}$ cup sesame seeds
- 110 grams/4 ounces/1 cup plain (all-purpose) flour
- 1 egg, beaten
- cooking oil for deep-frying
- lettuce, torn into large pieces
- yam bean, peeled and sliced
- cucumber, sliced
- Mango Sauce*

Method

1. Combine the crabmeat, potato, bread, chilli, mayonnaise, tom yam paste, kaffir lime leaf or *kesum* leaves and salt.
2. In a separate bowl, mix together the breadcrumbs and sesame seeds.
3. Shape the crabmeat mixture into balls. Coat the balls with flour, dip them into beaten egg and roll them in the breadcrumb and sesame seed mixture.
4. Deep-fry over medium heat until golden brown. Drain and arrange on a serving dish.
5. Garnish with lettuce, yam bean and cucumber.
6. Serve with Mango Sauce.

*MANGO SAUCE

Ingredients

- 3 tablespoons custard powder
- 250 ml/8 fl oz/1 cup water
- 1 ripe mango, peeled and puréed
- 1 red chilli, minced
- 1 tablespoon chopped coriander leaves (cilantro)
- 1 tablespoon lime juice
- salt
- sugar

Method

1. Blend the custard powder and water. Add the mango.
2. Add the remaining ingredients and bring the sauce to a boil. If it becomes too thick, add a bit more water.

Opposite: Thai Pineapple Prawn (Shrimp) Curry.

KERALA COCONUT PRAWNS (SHRIMPS)

Ingredients

85 grams/3 ounces/³/₈ cup ghee

1 teaspoon mustard seeds

3 sprigs + 2 sprigs curry leaves

1 onion, peeled and cut into rings

5 cloves garlic, peeled and minced

1 tablespoon peeled, minced ginger

2 tablespoons powdered chilli

1 teaspoon powdered turmeric

3 green chillies

handful of white grated coconut

700 grams/1¹/₂ pounds medium prawns (shrimps), legs and feelers removed

salt

sugar

2 teaspoons lime juice

Roasted and Pounded Spices

2 tablespoons coriander seeds

1 teaspoon fennel seeds

1 teaspoon black peppercorns

Method

1. Heat the ghee and fry the mustard seeds and 3 sprigs curry leaves until the seeds start to pop. Add the onion, garlic and ginger. Sauté until golden.

2. Add the roasted and pounded spices, powdered chilli, turmeric and green chillies. Sauté until fragrant.

3. Add the coconut, stir well and then add the prawns (shrimps).

4. Stir until the prawns (shrimps) are cooked and remove from heat. Season with salt and sugar. Add lime juice.

5. Just before serving, garnish with the remainig curry leaves.

KETAM GORENG ISTIMEWA
(Special Fried Chilli Crab)

Ingredients

60 ml/2 fl oz/¹/₄ cup cooking oil

8 red chillies, pounded

6 cloves garlic, peeled and finely chopped

2 tablespoons oyster sauce

1 teaspoon light soy sauce

60 ml/2 fl oz/¹/₄ cup chilli sauce

2 tablespoons canned tomato sauce

6 large crabs, halved

250 ml/8 fl oz/1 cup chicken stock

140 grams/5 ounces/1 cup bamboo shoots, finely sliced

4 shiitake mushrooms, halved

3 spring onions (scallions), coarsely sliced

¹/₂ onion, peeled and finely sliced

3 eggs, beaten

125 ml/4 fl oz/¹/₂ cup coconut milk, extracted from 1 grated coconut and 125 ml/4 fl oz/¹/₂ cup water

salt

sugar

Method

1. Heat the oil and sauté the chillies and garlic until fragrant.

2. Add the oyster sauce, soy sauce, chilli sauce, tomato sauce and crabs. Stir-fry for about 10 minutes, until the crabs change colour.

3. Pour in the chicken stock and simmer until the gravy thickens.

4. Add the bamboo shoots, mushrooms, spring onions (scallions) and onion and simmer until cooked.

5. Pour in the beaten egg and coconut milk and stir thoroughly. Season with salt and sugar, bring to a boil and remove from heat.

SPICY TOM YAM FRIED CRAB

Ingredients

4 large crabs, halved

freshly cracked white pepper

2 tablespoons cornflour (cornstarch)

2 eggs, beaten separately

2 teaspoons sugar

cooking oil for deep-frying

3 tablespoons butter

4 shallots, peeled and finely chopped

2 cloves garlic, peeled

1 tablespoon peeled, finely chopped ginger

2 tablespoons tom yam paste

6 bird's eye chillies, finely sliced

1 tablespoon soy sauce

handful of coriander leaves (cilantro), chopped

Method

1. Mix together the crabs, pepper, cornflour (cornstarch), 1 egg and 1 teaspoon sugar. Deep-fry in hot oil. Drain and set aside.

2. Heat the butter and fry the shallots, garlic, ginger and tom yam paste. Add the chillies, fried crabs, soy sauce and remaining 1 teaspoon sugar.

3. Quickly stir in the remaining egg and cook until done.

4. Just before serving, garnish with coriander leaves (cilantro).

Opposite: Kerala Coconut Prawns (Shrimps).

SNAPPER FILLET PICCATTA

Ingredients

2 (300 grams/10^1/$_2$ ounces each) boneless red snapper or lemon sole fillets

salt

freshly cracked black pepper

1 tablespoon plain (all-purpose) flour

2 tablespoons butter

2 tablespoons olive oil

2 tablespoons capers

125 ml/4 fl oz/^{1}/$_2$ cup fish stock or chicken stock or white wine

1 tablespoon lemon juice

2 tablespoons chopped parsley

lemon, sliced

Method

1. Season the fish with salt and pepper. Dust with flour.

2. Melt 1 tablespoon butter in the oil until it starts to sizzle. Add the fish fillets and fry about 3 minutes on each side until lightly browned. Add the capers and shake the pan for a few minutes. Remove the fish fillets and place them on a serving dish.

3. Deglaze the pan with the stock or wine and lemon juice. Swirl the pan and let the sauce simmer.

4. Remove from heat, add the remaining 1 tablespoon butter and swirl the pan until the butter melts. Be careful not to let the butter separate from the sauce.

5. Pour the sauce over the fish fillets, sprinkle with parsley and garnish with lemon slices.

6. Serve immediately.

Note: This dish goes well with mashed potato.

STIR-FRIED PRAWNS (SHRIMPS) WITH PINEAPPLE

Ingredients

3 tablespoons peanut oil

4 cloves garlic, peeled and minced

350 grams/12 ounces medium prawns (shrimps), shelled and deveined

^{1}/$_2$ ripe pineapple, finely diced

^{1}/$_2$ green capsicum (bell pepper), finely diced

^{1}/$_2$ red capsicum (bell pepper), finely diced

2 tablespoons white vinegar

2 tablespoons sugar

1 teaspoon cornflour (cornstarch), mixed with 60 ml/2 fl oz/^{1}/$_4$ cup chicken stock

3 spring onions (scallions), cut into 2-cm/1-inch lengths

handful of coriander leaves (cilantro), chopped

Method

1. Heat the oil and fry the garlic and prawns (shrimps). Add the pineapple and green and red capsicums (bell peppers) and stir-fry over high heat.

2. Add the vinegar, sugar and cornflour (cornstarch) mixture. When the sauce thickens, add the spring onions (scallions).

3. Serve immediately, garnished with coriander leaves (cilantro).

SAFFRON SQUID WITH TOMATO

Ingredients

60 ml/2 fl oz/^{1}/$_4$ cup extra virgin olive oil

600 grams/1 pounds, 5 ounces squid, cut into large pieces

^{1}/$_2$ onion, peeled and minced

4 cloves garlic, peeled and minced

125 ml/4 fl oz/^{1}/$_2$ cup fish stock or white wine

2 potatoes, peeled and finely sliced

1 can (411 grams/14^1/$_2$ ounces) Italian plum tomatoes, mashed

125 ml/4 fl oz/^{1}/$_2$ cup water (optional)

1 teaspoon saffron strands

6 sprigs (Western) basil leaves, finely sliced

salt

freshly cracked black pepper

1 tablespoon chopped parsley

Method

1. Heat the oil and fry the squid. Drain and set aside.

2. In the same oil, sauté the onion and garlic. Add the fish stock or wine and cook until the liquid is reduced to half its volume.

3. Add the potatoes, tomatoes and water (optional). Simmer until the potato is done.

4. When the sauce thickens, stir in the saffron, basil leaves and fried squid. Season with salt and pepper. Remove from heat and serve immediately, garnished with parsley.

MASALA PRAWNS (SHRIMPS)

Ingredients

- 1 kilogram/2 pounds, 3 ounces large prawns (shrimps), shelled and deveined
- 3 tablespoons ghee
- 10 shallots, peeled and finely sliced
- 1 tablespoon powdered chilli
- 1 tablespoon powdered fennel
- 1 tablespoon ground black pepper
- 3 tablespoons canned tomato sauce
- 3 tablespoons grated coconut
- 2 tablespoons tamarind juice, extracted from 1 tablespoon tamarind pulp and 2 tablespoons water
- salt
- sugar
- handful of coriander leaves (cilantro), chopped

Marinade (finely ground)

- 4 cloves garlic, peeled
- 10 shallots, peeled
- 1 cm/^{1}/$_2$ inch ginger, peeled
- 1 cm/^{1}/$_2$ inch fresh turmeric, peeled

Method

1. Combine the prawns (shrimps) with the marinade and set aside for 30 minutes.
2. Heat the ghee and fry the shallots until fragrant.
3. Add the chilli, fennel and pepper and stir-fry briefly. Add the marinated prawns (shrimps), tomato sauce, coconut, tamarind juice, salt and sugar. Stir until the prawns (shrimps) are cooked.
4. Just before serving, garnish with coriander leaves (cilantro).

LALA TUMIS PEDAS
(Chilli Fried Clams)

Ingredients

- 60 ml/2 fl oz/^{1}/$_4$ cup peanut oil
- 2 stalks lemon grass, bruised
- 2 tablespoons yellow or black *tau cheo* (preserved soy beans)
- 2 tablespoons oyster sauce
- 500 grams/1 pound, 1^1/$_2$ ounces clams, washed and drained
- 250 ml/8 fl oz/1 cup fish stock or water
- 1 teaspoon cornflour (cornstarch), mixed with 1 tablespoon water
- 6 spring onions (scallions), cut into 2-cm/1-inch lengths
- ^{1}/$_2$ teaspoon sugar
- red chilli, sliced

Finely Pounded Paste

- 5 red chillies
- 4 cloves garlic, peeled
- 2 cm/1 inch ginger, peeled

Method

1. Heat the oil and sauté the lemon grass and finely pounded paste until fragrant.
2. Add the *tau cheo*, oyster sauce and clams. Stir well and cover tightly.
3. After 2–3 minutes remove the lid and make sure that all the clams have opened. Stir in the fish stock or water, cornflour (cornstarch) mixture and spring onions (scallions). Season with sugar and bring the gravy to a simmer.
4. When the gravy thickens, remove from heat.
5. Serve immediately, garnished with chilli.

Note: Make sure that the clams are not overcooked. They must be juicy and moist. The secret is to have all the ingredients ready when you start cooking, and to prepare this dish last of all before serving.

SELADA UDANG RAMPAI
(Hot and Tangy Prawns [Shrimps])

Ingredients

- 60 ml/2 fl oz/^{1}/$_4$ cup cooking oil
- 1 cm/^{1}/$_2$ inch ginger, peeled and pounded
- 2 cloves garlic, peeled and pounded
- 1 teaspoon mustard seeds
- 2 tablespoons powdered chilli
- 2 teaspoons powdered turmeric
- 2 tablespoons vinegar
- salt
- sugar
- ^{1}/$_2$ cucumber, sliced
- ^{1}/$_2$ carrot, peeled and sliced
- 1 green chilli, halved lengthways
- 1 red chilli, halved lengthways
- 1 onion, peeled and coarsely sliced
- 3 cloves garlic, peeled and halved
- 10 large prawns (shrimps), legs and feelers removed

Method

1. Heat the oil and sauté the pounded ginger and garlic until fragrant.
2. Stir in the mustard seeds and add the powdered chilli, turmeric, vinegar, salt and sugar.
3. Add the cucumber, carrot, green and red chillies, onion, garlic and prawns (shrimps). Stir-fry until cooked.

Opposite: Lala Tumis Pedas (Chilli Fried Clams).

SAMBAL SOTONG KERING EMAK
(Mother's Dried Squid in Chilli Sauce)

When I was a child my mother cooked this sambal once a month, on my father's pay day. Dried squid was expensive in those days, and this dish was a special treat for our family. Dried squid normally has to be soaked in *air kapur* (alkaline water) overnight before cooking, but these days in some places it can be bought ready to cook. I love the flavour of the peanuts as well as the sweetness of this sambal. It tastes wonderful with nasi lemak.

Ingredients

- 90 ml/3 fl oz/³/₈ cup cooking oil
- 4 large dried squid, soaked in *air kapur* (alkaline water) overnight, drained and cut into bite-sized pieces
- salt
- sugar
- 60 ml/2 fl oz/¹/₄ cup water
- 375 ml/12 fl oz/1¹/₂ cups tamarind juice, extracted from 2¹/₂ tablespoons tamarind pulp and 375 ml/12 fl oz/1¹/₂ cups water
- 170 grams/6 ounces/1 cup peanuts, roasted and coarsely pounded

Finely Ground Paste

- 40 dried chillies, seeded, soaked in water and drained
- 1 teaspoon shrimp paste
- 15 shallots, peeled

Method

1. Heat the oil over medium heat and sauté the finely ground paste until the oil separates and the mixture is fragrant.
2. Add the squid, salt, sugar and water. Simmer for 20 minutes until the squid is soft. Add the tamarind juice and peanuts. Cook until the gravy thickens.

KENUS MEBASE
(Squid Curry)

Ingredients

- 3 tablespoons cooking oil
- 250 ml/8 fl oz/1 cup chicken stock
- 3 *salam* leaves
- 250 ml/8 fl oz/1 cup coconut milk, extracted from ¹/₂ grated coconut and 250 ml/8 fl oz/1 cup water
- 2 red chillies, sliced
- 1 green chilli, sliced
- 500 grams/1 pound, 1¹/₂ ounces squid, cut into rings
- salt
- sugar
- lime juice

Finely Ground Paste

- 8 red chillies
- 3 bird's eye chillies
- 1 tablespoon coriander seeds, roasted
- 1 teaspoon shrimp paste
- 6 candlenuts
- 4 cloves garlic, peeled
- 1 cm/¹/₂ inch *cekur* (lesser galangal), peeled
- 1 cm/¹/₂ inch galangal, peeled
- 2 cm/1 inch fresh turmeric, peeled
- 2 stalks lemon grass, finely sliced
- 2 tablespoons grated palm sugar or brown sugar
- 2 *salam* leaves

Method

1. Heat the oil and sauté the finely ground paste until fragrant.
2. Add the chicken stock and *salam* leaves and boil for a few minutes.
3. Add the coconut milk, red and green chillies and squid. Cook for 1–2 minutes until the squid is done. Season with salt, sugar and lime juice.

THAI PINEAPPLE SEAFOOD CURRY

Ingredients

- 60 ml/2 fl oz/¹/₄ cup peanut oil
- 4 shallots, peeled and sliced
- 3 tablespoons Thai red curry paste
- 750 ml/1¹/₅ pints/3 cups coconut milk, extracted from 1 grated coconut and 750 ml/1¹/₅ pints/3 cups water
- 1 stalk lemon grass, bruised
- 2 kaffir lime leaves
- 140 grams/5 ounces/1 cup diced pineapple
- 3 tablespoons *nam pla*
- 1¹/₂ tablespoons sugar
- 100 grams/3¹/₂ ounces prawns (shrimps), legs and feelers removed
- 100 grams/3¹/₂ ounces squid, cut into rings
- 200 grams/7 ounces snapper fillet, diced
- juice of 1 lime

Method

1. Heat the oil and sauté the shallots until golden. Add the Thai red curry paste and fry until fragrant. Pour in the coconut milk and bring to a simmer.
2. Add the lemon grass, kaffir lime leaves and pineapple. Simmer for 10 minutes. Add the *nam pla*, sugar, prawns, squid and fish. Stir in the lime juice and bring to a simmer.

Opposite: Kenus Mebase (Squid Curry).

RENDANG KERANG
(Cockle Rendang)

Ingredients

60 ml/2 fl oz/$^1/_4$ cup cooking oil

1 litre/1$^3/_5$ pints/4 cups coconut milk, extracted from 1$^1/_2$ grated coconuts and 1 litre/1$^3/_5$ pints/4 cups water

3 pieces *asam gelugur*

1 turmeric leaf, finely sliced

1 kaffir lime leaf, finely sliced

600 grams/1 pounds, 5 ounces cockle meat

salt

sugar

55 grams/2 ounces/$^1/_2$ cup *kerisik* (pounded roasted grated or desiccated coconut)

Finely Ground Paste

10 dried chillies, seeded, soaked in water and drained

5 bird's eye chillies

2 stalks lemon grass, finely sliced

5 shallots, peeled

1 clove garlic, peeled

1 cm/$^1/_2$ inch ginger, peeled

1 cm/$^1/_2$ inch galangal, peeled

1 cm/$^1/_2$ inch fresh turmeric, peeled

Method

1. Heat the oil and sauté the finely ground paste until almost dry.

2. Pour in the coconut milk and add the *asam gelugur*, turmeric leaf and kaffir lime leaf. Simmer until the gravy thickens.

3. Add the cockle meat and season with salt and sugar. Simmer until the cockle meat is cooked.

4. Add the *kerisik* and simmer for 5 minutes over medium heat.

KALIO UDANG TEMPOYAK
(Prawns [Shrimps] in Preserved Durian Gravy)

Ingredients

1 stalk lemon grass, bruised

750 ml/1$^1/_5$ pints/3 cups coconut milk, extracted from 1 grated coconut and 750 ml/1$^1/_5$ pints/3 cups water

125 grams/4$^1/_2$ ounces/$^1/_2$ cup *tempoyak* (preserved salted durian)

salt

sugar

1 tomato, quartered

500 grams/1 pound, 1$^1/_2$ ounces freshwater prawns (shrimps), legs and feelers removed

Finely Ground Paste

5 bird's eye chillies

4 red chillies

1 cm/$^1/_2$ inch fresh turmeric, peeled

4 candlenuts

8 shallots, peeled

2 cloves garlic, peeled

Method

1. Combine the finely ground paste, lemon grass and coconut milk in a pot. Simmer for 5–7 minutes.

2. Add the *tempoyak*, salt, sugar and tomato. Bring to a boil.

3. Stir in the prawns (shrimps) and simmer for 3 minutes.

RENDANG UDANG HARIMAU
(Tiger Prawn Rendang)

Ingredients

60 ml/2 fl oz/$^1/_4$ cup cooking oil

500 ml/16 fl oz/2 cups coconut milk, extracted from 1 grated coconut and 500 ml/16 fl oz/2 cups water

2.5 cm/1 inch cinnamon stick

3 star anise

5 cloves

3 kaffir lime leaves

55 grams/2 ounces/$^1/_2$ cup *kerisik* (pounded roasted grated or desiccated coconut)

1 kilogram/2 pounds, 3 ounces tiger prawns, legs and feelers removed, deep-fried for 3 minutes and drained

Finely Ground Paste

4 tablespoons chilli paste

3 candlenuts

15 shallots, peeled

4 cloves garlic, peeled

3 stalks lemon grass, finely sliced

1 cm/$^1/_2$ inch fresh turmeric, peeled

1 cm/$^1/_2$ inch galangal, peeled

1 cm/$^1/_2$ inch ginger, peeled

Method

1. Heat the oil and sauté the finely ground paste until fragrant.

2. Add the coconut milk, cinnamon, star anise, cloves and lime leaves. Bring to a boil and simmer until the gravy thickens.

3. Add the *kerisik* and prawns (shrimps) and continue to simmer until the oil separates and gravy is slightly dry.

Note: This rendang can be served with rice, bread or ketupat (rice cake).

Opposite: Rendang Kerang (Cockle Rendang).

VEGETABLES

156

Sayur Asam Bandung
(Vegetables in Sweet and Sour Gravy)

Peria Lemak Udang
(Rich Prawn [Shrimp] with
Bitter Gourd)

Thai Mushroom Curry

158

Lemak Kentang dan Dhal
(Potato and Dhal [Split Peas] in Coconut Gravy)

Imam Balidi

150

Vegetable Curry

Moroccan Meat-Stuffed Capsicums
(Bell Peppers)

152

Acar Rempah
(Curry Pickle)

Ratatouille
(South of France Mixed Vegetable Stew)

Stir-Fried Lady's Fingers (Okra)
with Minced (Ground) Beef

154

Lemak Lodeh
(Mixed Vegetables in Coconut Gravy)

Cili Sumbat Berkuah Santan
(Stuffed Chilli in Coconut Gravy)

I've always believed that good nutrition is nothing more nor less than good food properly selected and carefully prepared. When it comes to eating, one can indulge at times but one must be disciplined. During my schooldays I was active, fit and alert. That does not mean I was the perfect child. Sometimes I drowned myself in ice cream, sweets and nuts, like any growing kid, but I usually tried to eat well. This meant having three balanced meals a day—and, yes, I finished all the vegetables on my plate!

By the way, did your mother keep reminding you to eat your vegetables? Well, she was right. Not only are vegetables good sources of vitamins and minerals, they also contain fibre, protein and complex carbohydrates. Best of all, except for the starchy ones—sweet potatoes, pumpkins, etc.—vegetables are low in calories. Even potatoes, which have been falsely maligned over the years, are a good source of fibre and vitamin C.

One important thing to remember about vegetables is that they shouldn't be overcooked—never mind what the French chef says! Attitudes towards cooking have changed dramatically over the years. Today the emphasis is on preserving the natural goodness of vegetables by cooking them for the shortest time possible, just until tender with a slight suggestion of crunchiness.

I've often been asked by home cooks, through mail or at my live cook shows, how to cook vegetables so that they look green and glossy like in Chinese restaurants. Many of our vegetables at home turn out dull, grey and soggy. Besides knowing how to select vegetables at their best, it is important to choose the correct technique of preparing them. If they are prepared correctly, not only do they retain their colour, flavour, shape and texture, they also maintain their nutrients. Back to how my leafy vegetables stay green during stir-frying—before stir-frying them, I normally blanch them in a pot of boiling water and immediately cool them under running cold water to refresh them. This not only keeps the vegetables green but stops the cooking process immediately. I add these vegetables last of all to the stir-fried dish.

Stir-frying utilises high heat and a short cooking time to produce vegetables with a tender-crisp texture, bright colour and rich natural flavour. Whether you stir-fry in a wok or a frying pan, the basic procedure is the same. Fry the vegetables quickly—uncovered, of course. This will help the liquid evaporate quickly. If you need some sauce with the vegetables, just add water or stock and perhaps thicken the sauce with a little bit of cornflour (cornstarch).

V
E
G
E
T
A
B
L
E
S

I usually parboil vegetables that take longer to cook and either blanch leafy vegetables or directly stir-fry them in the wok. There are many ways vegetables can be cooked and presented in an appetising manner. I think one of the reasons many of us don't care to eat vegetables is because we don't know how to prepare them in an interesting way. Besides stir-frying, steaming and baking them—along with roast meat, for instance—you can stuff them, purée them, deep-fry them, boil them in soups and stews or have them raw in salads. In fact, whenever I make a stew I try to incorporate plenty of vegetables, such as carrot, capsicum (bell pepper), tomato and celery. In this way I get a well-balanced, nutritious meal in one dish.

When preparing vegetables, keep in mind their colour, texture and taste so that they balance and enhance the other dishes you are serving. It would be dreadfully dull to face a dinner plate on which everything was pale, white or of uniformly soft consistency.

Careful selection of green vegetables is important. *Jangan asyik nak beli longok dipasar* (Don't buy them in little heaps) at the market just because they are cheap. In fact, it's worth going out of your way to find a stall in a produce market that supplies pesticide-free and organic vegetables. They may not look as perfect, but at least you know that they are safe and have been grown in a natural manner. Whenever possible, try to get fresh rather than canned or frozen vegetables. Buy them when they are in season: they are less expensive and also at their best. Try to buy vegetables shortly before you plan to use them, and do not buy more than you need. In fact, how about trying to grow some in your own backyard?

Some vegetables may simply be washed and steamed or baked. These methods of cooking keep vitamin loss to a minimum, provided the cooking time is not too long. Often, vegetables are scrubbed, scraped or thinly peeled before cooking. Remember that most vitamins lie near the skin and that deep peeling thus causes a loss of nutrients. Prepared, peeled vegetables should be cooked immediately, to minimise their exposure to air. Do not soak vegetables in water after slicing them, to preserve their nutrients. Whether you cook vegetables whole or sliced, make sure that the pieces are uniform in size so that they cook simultaneously.

This chapter includes some of my interesting ways of preparing vegetables. Several of the recipes are so delicious that once you have tried them out, you may decide to turn vegetarian. Given the current woes plaguing pigs, chickens and cows, that may not be such a bad idea!

VEGETABLE CURRY

Ingredients

60 ml/2 fl oz/$^1/_4$ cup corn oil

$^1/_2$ teaspoon cumin seeds

1 onion, peeled and diced

2 green chillies, chopped

1 cm/$^1/_2$ inch ginger, peeled and finely chopped

3 cloves garlic, peeled and finely chopped

$^1/_4$ teaspoon powdered turmeric

1 tablespoon powdered coriander

$^1/_2$ teaspoon powdered chilli

250 ml/8 fl oz/1 cup tomato purée (tomato paste)

2 potatoes, peeled and cut into wedges

1 carrot, peeled and diced

20 French beans, cut into 4-cm/1$^3/_4$-inch lengths

2 tomatoes, cut into wedges

1 sprig coriander leaves (cilantro), chopped

salt

Method

1. Heat the oil and sauté the cumin seeds, onion and green chillies for 3 minutes. Add the ginger, garlic, powdered turmeric, coriander and chilli and fry until fragrant. Mix in the tomato purée (tomato paste) and cook for 5 minutes.

2. Add the potatoes and cook for 5 minutes. Add the carrot and French beans and cook for another 3 minutes.

3. Add the tomatoes, coriander leaves (cilantro) and salt. Cook uncovered, over low heat, until the vegetables are tender.

MOROCCAN MEAT-STUFFED CAPSICUMS (BELL PEPPERS)

Ingredients

3 red capsicums (bell peppers)

3 yellow capsicums (bell peppers)

3 tablespoons olive oil

2 onions, peeled and finely diced

300 grams/10$^1/_2$ ounces minced mutton (ground lamb)

1 teaspoon powdered turmeric

1 tablespoon chopped fresh tarragon

1 teaspoon chopped fresh dill

2 fresh bay leaves

3 tablespoons tomato purée (tomato paste)

140 grams/5 ounces/1$^1/_4$ cup spring onions (scallions), finely chopped

140 grams/5 ounces/2$^1/_2$ cup coriander leaves (cilantro), finely chopped

450 grams/1 pound/2 cups rice, parboiled and drained

salt

freshly cracked black pepper

Tomato Sauce*

Method

1. Cut off the tops of the red and yellow capsicums (bell peppers) and remove the seeds. Reserve the tops.

2. Heat the oil and sauté the onions until soft. Stir in the mutton (lamb), turmeric, tarragon, dill and bay leaves. Fry for a few minutes.

3. Add the tomato purée (tomato paste), spring onions (scallions), coriander leaves (cilantro) and rice. Mix well and season with salt and pepper.

4. Spoon filling into the capsicums (bell peppers), replace the tops and arrange on a baking tray. Top with Tomato Sauce and bake in a 180°C/350°F preheated oven for 40 minutes.

5. Spoon the remaining sauce over the capsicums (bell peppers) and serve immediately.

*TOMATO SAUCE

Ingredients

5 tablespoons tomato ketchup

5 tablespoons chilli sauce

250 ml/8 fl oz/1 cup water

60 ml/2 fl oz/$^1/_4$ cup olive oil

2 tablespoons cider vinegar

Method

Mix all the ingredients in a saucepan and boil for 10 minutes.

Opposite: Moroccan Meat-stuffed Capsicums (Bell Peppers).

ACAR REMPAH
(Curry Pickle)

Ingredients

90 ml/3 fl oz/$^3/_8$ cup cooking oil

1 tablespoon fenugreek seeds

1 tablespoon mustard seeds

140 grams/5 ounces small prawns (shrimps), shelled and deveined

1 tablespoon dried prawns (shrimps), soaked in water, drained and pounded

2 tablespoons dried anchovies, washed and pounded

2 cucumbers, seeded, cut into 3-cm/1$^1/_2$-inch lengths, soaked in salt water and drained

2 carrots, peeled and cut into 3-cm/1$^1/_2$-inch lengths

2 green chillies, halved lengthways

2 red chillies, halved lengthways

2 onions, peeled and quartered

2 tablespoons *kerisik* (pounded roasted grated or desiccated coconut)

60 ml/2 fl oz/$^1/_4$ cup white vinegar

salt

sugar

Whole Spices

6 cardamoms

6 star anise

2 cm/1 inch cinnamon stick

Finely Ground Paste

1 teaspoon shrimp paste

10 shallots, peeled

6 cloves garlic, peeled

2 cm/1 inch fresh turmeric, peeled

2 cm/1 inch ginger, peeled

Roasted and Finely Ground Spices

30 grams/1 ounce/$^1/_4$ cup coriander seeds

2 tablespoons fennel seeds

1 tablespoon black peppercorns

2 star anise

Method

1. Heat the oil and sauté the fenugreek seeds, mustard seeds, whole spices and finely ground paste until fragrant.

2. Stir in the fresh prawns (shrimps), dried prawns (shrimps) and dried anchovies and sauté for 2–3 minutes.

3. Add the cucumbers, carrots, green and red chillies, onions and roasted ground spices. Stir for 7 minutes.

4. Add the *kerisik* and vinegar. Season with salt and sugar and cook for 5 minutes.

Note: It is best to prepare this pickle a day in advance.

RATATOUILLE
(South of France Mixed Vegetable Stew)

Ingredients

90 ml/3 fl oz/$^3/_8$ cup olive oil

1 large eggplant, diced

2 zucchini, diced

1 onion, peeled and diced

1 teaspoon chopped fresh thyme

1 teaspoon chopped (Western) basil leaves

1 green capsicum (bell pepper), diced

1 red capsicum (bell pepper), diced

3 cloves garlic, peeled and chopped

1 can (411 grams/14$^1/_2$ ounces) Italian plum tomatoes, mashed

1 tablespoon tomato purée (tomato paste)

salt

freshly cracked black pepper

sugar

Method

1. Heat the oil and sauté the eggplant and zucchini until the eggplant is soft. Add the onion, thyme, basil, green and red capsicums (bell peppers) and garlic. Sauté for another 3 minutes.

2. Add the tomatoes and tomato purée (tomato paste) and season with salt, pepper and sugar. Simmer over low heat until the vegetables are tender.

STIR-FRIED LADY'S FINGERS (OKRA) WITH MINCED (GROUND) BEEF

Ingredients

60 ml/2 fl oz/$^1/_4$ cup vegetable oil

250 grams/9 ounces minced (ground) beef

300 grams/10$^1/_2$ ounces lady's fingers (okra), stemmed and thickly sliced

1 red capsicum (bell pepper), sliced

2 tablespoons light soy sauce

1 teaspoon sugar

Finely Ground Paste

6 red chillies

2 teaspoons shrimp paste

4 cloves garlic, peeled

6 shallots, peeled

Method

1. Heat the oil and sauté the finely ground paste until fragrant. Add the beef and sauté until it changes colour.

2. Add the lady's fingers (okra) and capsicum (bell pepper) and season with soy sauce and sugar. Stir-fry until the vegetables are tender.

Opposite: Acar Rempah (Curry Pickle).

LEMAK LODEH
(Mixed Vegetables in Coconut Gravy)

Ingredients

90 ml/3 fl oz/$^3/_8$ cup cooking oil

1–1.25 litres/1$^3/_5$–2 pints/4–5 cups coconut milk, extracted from 1$^1/_2$ grated coconuts and 1–1.25 litres/1$^3/_5$–2 pints/4–5 cups water

4 *salam* leaves

1 carrot, peeled and cut into 2.5-cm/1-inch lengths

10 long beans, cut into 2.5-cm/1-inch lengths

2 potatoes, peeled and diced

$^1/_2$ cabbage, coarsely chopped

2 eggplants, sliced into rounds

3 green chillies, halved lengthways

3 red chillies, halved lengthways

55 grams/2 ounces/1$^1/_4$ cups glass noodles, soaked in water and drained

2 pieces bean curd, each cut into 6 pieces

2 pieces *tempe*, each cut into 6 pieces

4 pieces *fu chok* (bean curd skin), soaked in water and drained

salt

Finely Ground Paste

15 dried chillies, seeded, soaked in water and drained

1 tablespoon powdered coriander

8 candlenuts

2 stalks lemon grass, finely sliced

10 shallots, peeled

4 cloves garlic, peeled

55 grams/2 ounces/$^1/_2$ cup dried prawns (shrimps), soaked in water and drained

1 cm/$^1/_2$ inch galangal, peeled

1 cm/$^1/_2$ inch fresh turmeric, peeled

Method

1. Heat the oil in a soup pot and sauté the finely ground paste until fragrant.

2. Add the coconut milk and *salam* leaves and bring to a simmer. Add the carrot and cook for 10 minutes, then add the long beans, potatoes, cabbage, eggplants and green and red chillies.

3. Add the glass noodles, bean curd, *tempe* and *fu chok* and simmer for 5 minutes. Season with salt.

CILI SUMBAT BERKUAH SANTAN
(Stuffed Chilli in Coconut Gravy)

Ingredients

3 tablespoons cooking oil

6 shallots, peeled and finely sliced

2 cloves garlic, peeled and finely sliced

1 cm/$^1/_2$ inch ginger, peeled and finely sliced

3 sprigs curry leaves

Stuffed Chillies*

1 teaspoon powdered chilli

$^1/_2$ teaspoon powdered turmeric

500 ml/16 fl oz/2 cups coconut milk, extracted from 1 grated coconut and 500 ml/16 fl oz/2 cups water

125 ml/4 fl oz/$^1/_2$ cup water

2 tomatoes, quartered

salt

juice of 1 lime

Method

1. Heat the oil and sauté the shallots, garlic, ginger and curry leaves until the shallots and garlic are golden. Add the Stuffed Chillies, powdered chilli and turmeric and fry until fragrant.

2. Add the coconut milk, water and tomatoes. Season with salt. Simmer for 10 minutes until the sauce thickens. Adjust the seasoning and finish by adding lime juice.

*STUFFED CHILLIES

Ingredients

8–10 green chillies, slit lengthways and seeded

cooking oil for shallow-frying

Filling (well combined)

200 grams/7 ounces boneless Spanish mackerel, minced (ground)

30 grams/1 ounce/$^1/_4$ cup dried prawns (shrimps), soaked in water, drained and pounded

1 onion, peeled and finely chopped

1 cm/$^1/_2$ inch ginger, peeled and finely chopped

2 tablespoons chopped coriander leaves (cilantro)

juice of $^1/_2$ lime

$^3/_4$ teaspoon salt

Method

Stuff the chillies with filling. Shallow-fry them for a few minutes on each side until slightly softened. Drain and set aside.

Opposite: Cili Sumbat Berkuah Santan (Stuffed Chilli in Coconut Gravy).

SAYUR ASAM BANDUNG
(Vegetables in Sweet and Sour Gravy)

Ingredients

4 or 5 pieces *asam gelugur*

2 litres/3^1/$_5$ pints/8 cups water

2 *salam* leaves

2 cm/1 inch galangal, peeled and bruised

85 grams/3 ounces/^{1}/$_2$ cup peanuts

^{1}/$_2$ pumpkin, peeled and cut into large pieces

100 grams/3^1/$_2$ ounces unripe papaya, peeled and sliced

140 grams/5 ounces young jackfruit, peeled, cut into bite-sized pieces, blanched in boiling water and drained

200 grams/7 ounces long beans, cut into 2.5-cm/1-inch lengths

4 ears young corn

salt

Finely Ground Paste

6 red chillies

1 teaspoon roasted shrimp paste

4 candlenuts

2 cloves garlic, peeled

4 shallots, peeled

1 tablespoon brown sugar

Method

1. In a pot, mix the finely ground paste with the *asam gelugur* and water. Add the *salam* leaves, galangal and peanuts and bring to a boil.

2. Add the pumpkin and papaya and boil for 10 minutes. Add the jackfruit, long beans and corn and boil for another 10 minutes until all the vegetables are tender.

3. Season with salt and check that the gravy is sour enough. If not, add some more *asam gelugur*.

Note: Chopped tomatoes can be added to increase the sourness of the dish.

PERIA LEMAK UDANG
(Rich Prawn [Shrimp] with Bitter Gourd)

Ingredients

3 tablespoons cooking oil

2 teaspoons *tau cheo* (preserved soy beans)

500 ml/16 fl oz/2 cups coconut milk, extracted from ^{1}/$_2$ grated coconut and 500 ml/16 fl oz/2 cups water

250 grams/9 ounces small prawns (shrimps), shelled and deveined

500 grams/1 pound, 1^1/$_2$ ounces bitter gourd, cored and cut into bite-sized pieces

salt

Finely Ground Paste

6 red chillies

^{1}/$_4$ teaspoon shrimp paste

^{1}/$_4$ teaspoon ground white pepper

5 shallots, peeled

3 cloves garlic, peeled

^{1}/$_4$ teaspoon tamarind pulp

1 teaspoon brown sugar

Method

1. Heat the oil and fry the finely ground paste until fragrant. Add the *tau cheo* and fry for another few minutes.

2. Pour in the coconut milk, add the prawns (shrimps) and bring to a simmer. Add the bitter gourd and simmer for 5 minutes. Season with salt and remove from heat.

THAI MUSHROOM CURRY

Ingredients

90 ml/3 fl oz/^{3}/$_8$ cup cooking oil

500 grams/1 pound, 1^1/$_2$ ounces/5 cups fresh oyster mushrooms

435 ml/14 fl oz/1^3/$_4$ cups water

4 kaffir lime leaves

1 stalk *kesum* leaves

10 red bird's eye chillies

500 ml/16 fl oz/2 cups coconut milk, extracted from 1 grated coconut and 500 ml/16 fl oz/2 cups water

2^1/$_2$ tablespoons *nam pla*

2 teaspoons salt

^{1}/$_2$ teaspoon ground white pepper

Finely Ground Paste

4 green chillies

20 bird's eye chillies

8 shallots, peeled

5 cloves garlic, peeled

2 coriander roots

rind of 1 small kaffir lime

2^1/$_2$ teaspoons powdered cumin

4 stalks lemon grass, finely sliced

1 cm/^{1}/$_2$ inch galangal, peeled

1 teaspoon shrimp paste

Method

1. Heat the oil and sauté the finely ground paste until fragrant.

2. Stir in the mushrooms and water and bring to a boil.

3. After 10 minutes, add the kaffir lime leaves, *kesum* leaves, chillies, coconut milk, *nam pla*, salt and pepper. Simmer until done.

Opposite: Peria Lemak Udang (Rich Prawn [Shrimp] with Bitter Gourd).

LEMAK KENTANG DAN KACANG DAL
(Potato and Dhal [Split Peas] in Coconut Gravy)

On my father's pay day we used to enjoy my mother's Sambal Sotong Kering Emak, but towards the middle or end of the month my mother created all sorts of recipes using eggs. This dish is very cheap, but it is full of nutrients from the dhal (split peas), potato and eggs. My mother says that's why I'm so plump!

Ingredients

- 1 litre/1³/₅ pints/4 cups second-squeeze coconut milk and 500 ml/16 fl oz/ 2 cups first-squeeze coconut milk, extracted from 1 grated coconut
- 10 carambola, halved lengthways
- 4 potatoes, peeled and cut into 6 pieces each
- 200 grams/7 ounces/1 cup dhal (split peas), boiled
- 6 duck eggs, hard-boiled and shelled
- salt

Finely Pounded Paste

- 20 dried chillies, seeded, soaked in water and drained
- 100 grams/3¹/₂ ounces dried anchovies
- 6 shallots, peeled
- 2 cm/1 inch fresh turmeric, peeled

Method

1. Put the finely pounded paste in a pot together with the second-squeeze coconut milk, carambola and potatoes. Bring to a boil. Add the dhal and boil for another 15 minutes.

2. Add the first-squeeze coconut milk and eggs. Simmer for 10 minutes and season with salt.

Note: The dried chillies can be substituted with bird's eye chillies if you prefer a hotter dish.

IMAM BALIDI

This stuffed eggplant, one of Turkey's popular dishes, is eaten cold as a first course. In the traditional recipe the dish is literally soaked in olive oil, but you can use less oil if you wish.

Ingredients

- 6 long, slim eggplants, halved lengthways
- olive oil for shallow-frying
- Filling*
- 250 ml/8 fl oz/1 cup canned tomato juice
- salt
- freshly cracked black pepper
- 2 tablespoons vinegar
- fresh parsley, chopped

Method

1. Sprinkle the eggplants with salt and leave in a colander for 30 minutes to degorge. Rinse and pat dry with paper towels. Set aside.

2. Heat the oil and shallow-fry the eggplants to seal them, until they are lightly browned. Drain.

3. Using a sharp knife, make a deep slit along the length of each eggplant half and spoon as much filling as possible into the slits. Lay the eggplants in a baking dish. Pour in the tomato juice and add salt, pepper and vinegar. Sprinkle with parsley.

4. Cover and bake in a 180°C/350°F preheated oven for about 45 minutes.

*FILLING

- 3 tablespoons extra virgin olive oil
- 4 large onions, peeled and finely sliced
- 5 cloves garlic, peeled and finely chopped
- 8 tomatoes, chopped
- 1 green capsicum (bell pepper), finely sliced (optional)
- 2 teaspoons sugar
- salt
- freshly cracked black pepper
- fresh parsley, finely chopped

Heat the oil and sauté the onions and garlic until soft. Add the tomatoes and capsicum (bell pepper) (optional). Season with sugar, salt and pepper. Simmer for about 15 minutes until the liquid reduces, then stir in the parsley.

Opposite: Imam Balidi.

NOODLES & PASTA

NOODLES & PASTA

NOODLES

One of the pleasures of eating at a hawker centre is the variety of noodles available. From the Indian Muslim stall's fried noodles, mee rebus, Penang laksa, fried kway teow to the Chinese fried Cantonese noodles, the choices are endless. Being a Malaysian, I've always felt that we are lucky to be surrounded by delicious food all the time.

Noodles, because of their length, signify long life and are always served on birthdays. My maternal grandmother never fails to prepare Nyonya mee sua on her birthday every year. She turned ninety this year, and despite the four major strokes she has suffered she is still alive and kicking.

Chinese noodles can be divided into two broad categories: dried and fresh. Each of these is made with a variety of ingredients in the dough: wheat flour, rice, plain (all-purpose) flour, egg, beans, to name a few. The dough can be factory made or rolled, kneaded, flattened and cut by hand.

Following are some of the most common types of noodles available.

Wheat Noodles and Egg Noodles

Wheat noodles are made of hard or soft wheat flour and water. These heavy yellow noodles are used mainly by the Hokkien Chinese. Malay and Indian cooks use them for mee rebus and mee goreng. If egg has been added, the noodles are usually called egg noodles. They can be bought fresh or dried and come in various shapes. The flat noodles are generally used in soups, while the rounded noodles are best for stir-frying. If fresh noodles are used, they should be immersed in boiling water for 2–3 minutes or until they are soft before serving. In the case of dried noodles, they have to be cooked according to the package instructions.

Rice Flour Noodles

Known as kway teow or sa hor fun, the wide, flat rice noodles have a creamy texture and mild flavour. They can be bought dried or fresh, in various shapes and thicknesses. Laksa noodles, also made from rice flour, are available both dried and fresh.

Dried Chinese Rice Vermicelli

Dried Chinese rice vermicelli, called beehoon, is a fine white noodle made from rice flour. It is used in soups or fried with meat, chicken or seafood. It needs to be soaked in boiling water for 2–3 minutes and strained before being fried.

Dried Green Mung Pea or Cellophane Noodles

Dried green mung pea noodles are known as tunghoon or suun. They are also called cellophane noodles or glass noodles for their transparent texture.

PASTA

Less than a decade ago, pasta mostly meant spaghetti and meatballs. It has come a long way since then, and now it is a favourite with cooks of all persuasions. Pasta is a food that has universal appeal. While macaroni and spaghetti have long been popular both in homes and in restaurants, more unusual forms of pasta have become symbolic of modern cuisine. Because pasta is such a simple compound—flour and eggs or flour and water—our attention is naturally drawn to what goes into the sauce or the stuffing, and we tend to take for granted the essential component of the dish, the pasta itself. This is unfortunate. If we do not clearly perceive the differences in varieties of pasta, if we cannot tell the good pasta from the bad, we will never master the vast range of expression of this most versatile and satisfying food.

All pasta (meaning 'paste' in Italian) is based on a starchy dough. There are two kinds of dough, one containing egg and the other eggless. They are more or less interchangeable. The simpler and probably the original form is eggless pasta made of hard wheat (durum) flour and water, a resilient dough that can withstand rolling and shaping by machine.

In the opinion of most cooks, egg pasta is superior to the eggless. It tastes best if it is made shortly before cooking. Soft flour is good for egg pasta, though durum flour or a mixture of wheat and non-wheat flours, such as buckwheat and rye, may be used. Both eggless and egg pasta are usually cooked by boiling in water. Cooked pasta is almost always finished with melted butter or olive oil before the sauce is added, so that it doesn't stick together. Cooked pasta may also be baked in a sauce, as in lasagne. Raw pasta dough is sometimes stuffed before being simmered in sauce, as in ravioli or tortellini. Occasionally fresh pasta is deep-fried, as in our wantans.

Lately, the Italian culinary influence has been so widespread that most pasta dishes are known by their Italian names. However, the practice of serving pasta as a main dish did not originate in Italy. In a typical Italian meal, a relatively light serving of pasta is wedged between the antipasti—a light first course—and the main course.

Pasta begins as a mass of dough, which is then thinned before being cut or shaped. The thinning process is accomplished by stretching, compressing or extruding, the methods that in turn give us the three basic categories of pasta.

In the case of stretched pasta, the dough is gradually flattened and thinned out into a sheet by hand, using a long, narrow, perfectly cylindrical rolling pin over a counter made preferably of wood. What makes the stretching method unique is that no downward pressure is exerted to flatten the dough. The dough is rolled into a long strip before it is cut into different shapes, e.g., ravioli, pappardelle and lasagne. When dry, it resembles tough leather. When cooked, stretched pasta draws sauce to its surface and holds it there.

Compressed pasta is made by squeezing out the dough. This type of pasta has a smoother surface, a stickier texture and less flavour absorption capacity than the hand-stretched variety.

When a mass of dough is forced through a perforated die, it produces extruded pasta. After extrusion, the pasta must be dried slowly, at carefully controlled temperatures, in special chambers. Extruded pasta requires machinery of industrial size and is therefore frequently referred to as factory made. Some common examples of this type are macaroni, rigatoni, fusilli, penne and conchiglie. Highquality factory-made pasta is as fine a product as the best home-made pasta.

Following are some of my favourite noodle and pasta dishes, which I have served to guests throughout my career and often with excellent comments. Master them and you will soon be dishing them out to your family and friends again and again.

KOISIMI NA KUNG
(Chiengmai Fried Noodles)

Ingredients

3 tablespoons cooking oil

3 cloves garlic, peeled and finely chopped

100 grams/3^1/$_2$ ounces boneless chicken, finely sliced

100 grams/3^1/$_2$ ounces prawns (shrimps), shelled and deveined

55 grams/2 ounces/^{1}/$_4$ cup button mushrooms

8 asparagus spears, cut into 10-cm/ 4-inch lengths

45 grams/1^1/$_2$ ounces/^{1}/$_4$ cup canned or fresh bamboo shoots, sliced

1 tablespoon oyster sauce

^{1}/$_4$ teaspoon ground black pepper

2 tablespoons light soy sauce

250 ml/8 fl oz/1 cup chicken stock

140 grams/5 ounces yellow noodles

1 tablespoon cornflour (cornstarch), mixed with 2 tablespoons water

1 spring onion (scallion), chopped

Method

1. Heat the oil and sauté the garlic, chicken, prawns (shrimps), mushrooms, asparagus and bamboo shoots.

2. Add the oyster sauce, pepper, soy sauce and chicken stock and bring to a boil.

3. Stir in the yellow noodles and pour in the cornflour (cornstarch) mixture. Mix well and boil for another 2 minutes.

4. Serve immediately, garnished with spring onion (scallion).

Note: Sliced tomatoes may be added with the yellow noodles, and sliced red chillies may be added for garnishing.

MI REBUS CIK ANI
(Cik Ani's Mee Rebus)

Ingredients

2 kilograms/4 pounds, 6 ounces yellow noodles, blanched just before serving

200 grams/7 ounces bean sprouts, blanched just before serving

Gravy*

4 pieces bean curd, deep-fried and cut into 6 pieces each

3 green chillies, sliced

2 red chillies, sliced

4 sprigs Chinese celery, sliced

4 spring onions (scallions), sliced

55 grams/2 ounces/^{1}/$_2$ cup crisp-fried shallots

3 eggs, hard-boiled, shelled and cut into wedges

6 *kalamansi*, halved

How to Serve

1. Put some yellow noodles in individual serving bowls. Top with bean sprouts.

2. Pour gravy over the noodles. Garnish with fried bean curd, green and red chillies, Chinese celery, spring onions (scallions), crisp-fried shallots, eggs and *kalamansi*.

*GRAVY

Ingredients

60 ml/2 fl oz/^{1}/$_4$ cup cooking oil

3 tablespoons meat curry powder

110 grams/4 ounces/^{1}/$_2$ cup *tau cheo* (preserved soy beans)

1 kilogram/2 pounds, 3 ounces beef, cut into small pieces

2.5 litres/4 pints/10 cups water

1 kilogram/2 pounds, 3 ounces sweet potatoes, boiled, peeled and mashed

2 cm/1 inch galangal, peeled and bruised

5 tomatoes, quartered

85 grams/3 ounces/^{1}/$_2$ cup peanuts, roasted and pounded

salt

sugar

Finely Pounded Paste

10 shallots, peeled

6 cloves garlic, peeled

1 cm/^{1}/$_2$ inch ginger, peeled

Method

1. Heat the oil and sauté the finely pounded paste until fragrant. Add the meat curry powder and *tau cheo* and sauté until fragrant.

2. Add the beef, water, sweet potatoes and galangal and boil for 20 minutes.

3. Add the tomatoes and peanuts and bring to a simmer. Season with salt and sugar.

Opposite: Koisimi Na Kung (Chiengmai Fried Noodles).

BAKED KWAY TEOW LAYERED WITH TUNA

Ingredients

55 grams/2 oz/$1/4$ cup butter

1 kilogram/2 pounds, 3 ounces kway teow

Rich Sauce*

Tuna Filling**

3 eggplants, finely sliced, brushed with cooking oil and grilled over glowing charcoal

140 grams/5 ounces/$1^1/4$ cups grated mozzarella cheese

Method

1. Grease a baking dish with butter. Form layers of kway teow, Rich Sauce, Tuna Filling, eggplant and cheese.

2. Repeat the layers, ending with a layer of cheese.

3. Bake in a 180°C/350°F preheated oven for 45 minutes until golden brown. Serve immediately.

*RICH SAUCE

Ingredients

1 litre/$1^3/5$ pints/4 cups milk

pinch of powdered nutmeg

pinch of powdered clove

2 fresh bay leaves

110 grams/4 ounces/$1/2$ cup butter

55 grams/2 ounces/$1/2$ cup plain (all-purpose) flour

salt

freshly cracked black pepper

Method

1. Bring the milk, nutmeg, clove and bay leaves to a boil. Simmer for 5 minutes. Strain and set aside.

2. In a clean pot, melt the butter and sauté the flour over medium heat for

2 minutes. Pour in the milk and cook, stirring constantly, until the sauce thickens. Season with salt and pepper.

**TUNA FILLING

Ingredients

60 ml/2 fl oz/$1/4$ cup olive oil

2 onions, peeled and diced

15 grams/$1/2$ ounce/$1/4$ cup finely chopped parsley

1 teaspoon chopped fresh thyme

3 cans (185 grams/$6^1/2$ ounces each) tuna, drained

salt

freshly cracked black pepper

Method

1. Heat the oil and sauté the onions, parsley and thyme for 2 minutes.

2. Add the tuna, salt and pepper. Sauté for another 5 minutes.

OHNOKAUKSWE
(Burmese Curry Noodles)

Ingredients

300 grams/$10^1/2$ ounces yellow noodles, blanched just before serving

1 piece fish cake, deep-fried and sliced

4 eggs, hard-boiled, shelled and halved

Gravy*

55 grams/2 ounces/$1/2$ cup crisp-fried shallots

3 limes, sliced

spring onions (scallions), chopped

coriander leaves (cilantro), chopped

Method

1. Put some yellow noodles in individual serving bowls and top with fish cake and egg.

2. Pour gravy over the noodles. Garnish with crisp-fried shallots, spring onions

(scallions), coriander leaves (cilantro) and serve with lime slices.

*GRAVY

Ingredients

1 chicken (1.5 kilograms/3 pounds, $4^1/2$ ounces), skinned and cut into small pieces

salt

1 tablespoon powdered turmeric

60 ml/2 fl oz/$1/4$ cup cooking oil

2 onions, peeled and finely sliced

6 cloves garlic, peeled and finely chopped

1 cm/$1/2$ inch ginger, peeled and finely chopped

1 tablespoon powdered chilli

1 litre/$1^3/5$ pints/4 cups coconut milk, extracted from $1^1/2$ grated coconuts and 1 litre/$1^3/5$ pints/4 cups water

1 litre/$1^3/5$ pints/4 cups water

$1/2$ teaspoon ground black pepper

handful of coriander leaves (cilantro), chopped

5 tablespoons *nam pla*

2 tablespoons sugar

140 grams/5 ounces/1 cup channa dhal flour, mixed with 250 ml/8 fl oz/1 cup water

85 grams/3 ounces/$1/2$ cup roasted peanuts, pounded

Method

1. Rub the chicken with salt and turmeric and marinate for 10 minutes.

2. Heat the oil and sauté the onions, garlic and ginger until soft. Add the marinated chicken and chilli and cook for 10 minutes until the chicken shrinks.

3. Pour in the coconut milk and water. Add the pepper and coriander leaves (cilantro) and boil for 20 minutes. Stir in the *nam pla*, sugar, channa dhal flour mixture and peanuts.

4. Boil for another 10 minutes. Season with salt.

Opposite: Ohnokaukswe (Burmese Curry Noodles).

VIETNAMESE NOODLES IN BEEF BALL SOUP

Ingredients

300 grams/10½ ounces Mekong rice sticks or kway teow, blanched just before serving

Beef Ball Soup*

1 onion, peeled and finely sliced

handful of coriander leaves (cilantro), chopped

handful of basil (*selasih*) leaves, chopped

60 ml/2 fl oz/¼ cup hoisin sauce

60 ml/2 fl oz/¼ cup chilli sauce

Method

1. Put some rice sticks or kway teow in individual serving bowls.

2. Top with Beef Ball Soup and garnish with onion, coriander leaves (cilantro) and basil leaves.

3. Serve the hoisin sauce and chilli sauce as dips for the beef balls.

*BEEF BALL SOUP

Ingredients

500 grams/1 pound, 1½ ounces chopped beef shin bones

2 cm/1 inch ginger, peeled

1 teaspoon salt

3 litres/4⅘ pints/12 cups water

2 star anise

2 onions, peeled and finely sliced

60 ml/2 fl oz/¼ cup *nam pla*

Beef Balls (combined and shaped into marble-sized balls)

500 grams/1 pound, 1½ ounces minced (ground) beef

2 teaspoons tapioca flour

1 teaspoon salt

2 teaspoons baking powder

Method

1. Put the bones, ginger, salt, water, star anise, onions and *nam pla* in a soup pot. Simmer over low heat for 3 hours.

2. Remove the bones, add the beef balls and simmer for another 10 minutes.

LAKSA SARAWAK
(Sarawak Laksa)

Ingredients

60 ml/2 fl oz/¼ cup vegetable oil

300 grams/10½ ounces small prawns (shrimps), shelled, deveined and minced (ground)

1 (1 kilogram/2 pounds, 3 ounces) chicken, quartered

2 tablespoons + 1 sprig finely chopped coriander leaves (cilantro)

2 litres/3⅕ pints/8 cups coconut milk, extracted from 2 grated coconuts and 2 litres/3⅕ pints/8 cups water

30 grams/1 ounce/¼ cup lightly roasted sesame seeds, ground

85 grams/3 ounces/½ cup peanuts, pounded

juice of 1 lime

salt

sugar

500 grams/1 pound, 1½ ounces laksa noodles or beehoon or yellow noodles, blanched just before serving

Dried Prawn (Shrimp) Sambal*

10 *kalamansi*, halved

Finely Ground Paste

15 shallots, peeled

6 cloves garlic, peeled

5 candlenuts

20 dried chillies, seeded, soaked in water and drained

2 cm/1 inch galangal, peeled

4 stalks lemon grass, finely sliced

½ teaspoon shrimp paste

Method

1. Heat the oil and sauté the finely ground paste until fragrant. Add the prawns (shrimps) and chicken and cook over low heat for 2 minutes.

2. Add 2 tablespoons coriander leaves (cilantro) and coconut milk and simmer for 30 minutes.

3. Add the sesame seeds, peanuts, lime juice, salt and sugar. Season well and serve hot with laksa noodles or beehoon or yellow noodles, the remaining coriander leaves (cilantro), Dried Prawn (Shrimp) Sambal and *kalamansi*.

Note: The laksa may be garnished with sliced red chillies and cucumber.

*DRIED PRAWN (SHRIMP) SAMBAL

Ingredients

3 tablespoons cooking oil

15 dried chillies, seeded, soaked in water, drained and pounded

6 shallots, peeled and pounded

55 grams/2 ounces/½ cup dried prawns (shrimps), soaked in water, drained and pounded

1 tablespoon tamarind juice, extracted from 1 teaspoon tamarind pulp and 1 tablespoon water

salt

sugar

Method

1. Heat the oil and sauté the chillies and shallots over low heat until fragrant.

2. Add the dried prawns (shrimps), tamarind juice, salt and sugar.

3. Cook the sambal until thick.

Opposite: Laksa Sarawak (Sarawak Laksa).

MACARONI PESCATORE

Ingredients

- 60 ml/2 fl oz/¼ cup olive oil
- 2 cloves garlic, peeled and finely chopped
- 300 grams/10½ ounces large prawns (shrimps), legs and feelers removed
- 200 grams/7 ounces boneless red snapper, diced
- 300 grams/10½ ounces squid, cut lengthways and scored diagonally
- 20 mussels
- Tomato Sauce*
- 125 ml/4 fl oz/½ cup thick prawn (shrimp) stock
- 500 grams/1 pound, 1½ ounces macaroni, boiled according to package instructions and drained
- 1 sprig parsley, finely chopped

Method

1. Heat the oil and sauté the garlic until fragrant. Add the prawns (shrimps), fish, squid and mussels.
2. Pour in the Tomato Sauce and prawn (shrimp) stock and simmer until the mussels open.
3. Pour the sauce over the macaroni and garnish with parsley.

*TOMATO SAUCE

- 60 ml/2 fl oz/¼ cup olive oil
- 1 teaspoon chopped fresh oregano
- 1 teaspoon chopped (Western) basil leaves
- 1 teaspoon chopped fresh thyme
- 2 cans (411 grams/14½ ounces each) Italian plum tomatoes, mashed
- 2 tablespoons tomato purée (tomato paste)
- 1 teaspoon sugar
- salt

Finely Ground Paste

- 1 onion, peeled
- 2 celery stalks, sliced
- 1 carrot, peeled and sliced
- 3 cloves garlic, peeled

Method

1. Heat the oil and sauté the finely ground paste, oregano, basil and thyme until fragrant.
2. Stir in the tomatoes and tomato purée (tomato paste) and simmer until the sauce thickens. Add the sugar and salt and simmer until cooked.

FRIED MACARONI FIESTA

Ingredients

- 55 grams/2 ounces/¼ cup ghee
- 100 grams/3½ ounces prawns (shrimps), shelled and deveined
- 100 grams/3½ ounces squid, cut into rings
- 200 grams/7 ounces fish fillet, cut into large cubes
- 60 ml/2 fl oz/¼ cup tomato ketchup
- 2 tablespoons oyster sauce
- 1 tablespoon sweet soy sauce
- salt
- sugar
- 100 grams/3½ ounces asparagus, cut into 4-cm/1¾-inch lengths
- 2 tomatoes, cut into wedges
- 250 ml/8 fl oz/1 cup chicken stock
- 300 grams/10½ ounces macaroni, boiled according to package instructions and drained
- handful of coriander leaves (cilantro), chopped
- 1 red chilli, finely sliced
- 500 grams/1 pound, 1½ ounces dried prawns (shrimps), fried and coarsely pounded

Pounded Paste

- 1 large onion, peeled
- 4 cloves garlic, peeled
- 1 teaspoon shrimp paste
- 2 tablespoons chilli paste

Method

1. Heat the ghee and sauté the pounded paste until fragrant.
2. Add the prawns (shrimps), squid, fish, tomato ketchup, oyster sauce and soy sauce. Season with salt and sugar. Sauté for a few minutes before adding the asparagus and tomatoes.
3. Add the chicken stock and macaroni and stir until the macaroni is coated in sauce. Garnish with coriander leaves (cilantro), chilli and dried prawns (shrimps).

Opposite: Macaroni Pescatore.

SPAGHETTI WITH MEATBALLS

Ingredients

85 ml/2^1/$_2$ fl oz/^{1}/$_3$ cup olive oil

1 onion, peeled and diced

4 cloves garlic, peeled and finely chopped

^{1}/$_2$ carrot, peeled and grated

1 celery stalk, finely diced

1 teaspoon chopped fresh oregano

1 teaspoon chopped fresh thyme

2 bay leaves

1 tablespoon tomato purée (tomato paste)

2 cans (411 grams/14^1/$_2$ ounces each) Italian plum tomatoes, mashed

2 bird's eye chillies, finely sliced

375 ml/12 fl oz/1^1/$_2$ cups water

salt

freshly cracked black pepper

sugar

500 grams/1 pound, 1^1/$_2$ ounces spaghetti, boiled according to package instructions and drained

Meatballs (combined and shaped into marble-sized balls)

500 grams/1 pound, 1^1/$_2$ ounces minced (ground) beef

^{1}/$_2$ onion, peeled and diced

2 slices white bread, soaked in 60 ml/ 2 fl oz/^{1}/$_4$ cup milk and mashed

1 tablespoon chopped parsley

salt

freshly cracked black pepper

Method

1. Heat the oil and sauté the onion, garlic, carrot, celery, oregano, thyme and bay leaves until fragrant.

2. Add the tomato purée (tomato paste) and stir-fry for a few minutes. Stir in the tomatoes and chillies.

3. Pour in the water and simmer for 20 minutes.

4. Add the meatballs and simmer for another 10 minutes. Season with salt, pepper and sugar.

5. Serve with spaghetti.

Note: Chopped fresh parsley may be sprinkled on top just before serving.

SPAGHETTI BOLOGNESE

Ingredients

60 ml/2 fl oz/^{1}/$_4$ cup olive oil

1 onion, peeled and finely chopped

4 cloves garlic, peeled and finely chopped

300 grams/10^1/$_2$ ounces minced (ground) beef

2 tablespoons tomato purée (tomato paste)

^{1}/$_2$ carrot, peeled and grated

^{1}/$_2$ celery stalk, grated

1 tablespoon chopped fresh oregano

1 teaspoon chopped fresh thyme

2 fresh bay leaves

3 tablespoons chopped parsley

1 can (411 grams/14^1/$_2$ ounces) Italian plum tomatoes, mashed

250 ml/8 fl oz/1 cup water

1 beef stock cube

salt

freshly cracked black pepper

sugar

500 grams/1 pound, 1^1/$_2$ ounces spaghetti, boiled according to package instructions and drained

grated Parmesan cheese

Method

1. Heat the oil and sauté the onion and garlic until soft. Add the beef and tomato purée (tomato paste) and sauté for 5 minutes. Add the carrot, celery, oregano, thyme, bay leaves and parsley and sauté for another 10 minutes.

2. Add the tomatoes, water and beef stock cube and simmer until the sauce thickens. Season with salt, pepper and sugar.

3. Pour the sauce over the spaghetti and sprinkle with cheese.

SPAGHETTI PUTTENESCA

Ingredients

60 ml/2 fl oz/^{1}/$_4$ cup olive oil

1 onion, peeled and diced

3 cloves garlic, peeled and finely chopped

1 teaspoon chopped fresh thyme

1 fresh bay leaf

1 can (411 grams/14^1/$_2$ ounces) Italian plum tomatoes, mashed

1 eggplant, diced

1 green capsicum (bell pepper), diced

1 red capsicum (bell pepper), diced

1 zucchini, diced

15 olives, pitted and sliced

3 tablespoons capers

3 salted fish or anchovy fillets

1 teaspoon powdered chilli

500 grams/1 pound, 1^1/$_2$ ounces spaghetti, boiled according to package instructions and drained

2 tablespoons chopped parsley

Method

1. Heat the oil and sauté the onion and garlic until soft. Add the thyme, bay leaf, tomatoes, eggplant, green and red capsicums (bell peppers), zucchini, olives, capers, salted fish or anchovy and chilli.

2. Cook for 20 minutes until the sauce thickens.

3. Pour the sauce over the spaghetti and garnish with parsley.

Opposite: Spaghetti with Meatballs.

SNACKS

Malaysians love snacking between meals. Be it a tea party or a *kenduri* (thanksgiving feast), we squeeze out the time for it. I've always enjoyed my family tradition of taking a tea break in the afternoon. These days, when I crave for something sweet and work leaves me with hardly any time to go out and buy a cake (let alone bake one—shame on me!), all I need to do is walk across the road near my home to Makcik Zah's stall for good goreng pisang (banana fritters).

On weekends, hotels are usually packed with guests at high tea receptions. I find that such gatherings lack a personal touch, as big groups often make it difficult to socialise. I've had tea with people who kept going to the buffet table fearing the food would finish if they didn't grab some more!

SNACKS

It is much more pleasant to chat with friends and family on a lazy Sunday afternoon in your own home and at your own pace. Fry some beehoon or kway teow or, if you like, make something unusual … try my Acaraje or Spanokopita.

For your child's next birthday party try the Mini Pizza or one of the delicious quiches. When planning a menu for the party, remember that children in groups tend not to eat very much. They seem to wear the food rather than put it in their stomachs. Have a colourful spread, with bite-sized snacks.

The snack recipes in this chapter are all equally delicious, and they're useful for just about any occasion.

TUNA PIZZA À LA MEDITERRANEAN

Ingredients

- 30 grams/1 ounce fresh yeast
- 180 ml/6 fl oz/$^3/_4$ cup lukewarm water
- 450 grams/1 pound/4 cups bread flour, sifted
- 1 teaspoon salt
- 1 teaspoon castor (super fine) sugar
- 2 tablespoons olive oil
- Tomato Sauce*

Toppings

- 2 tablespoon capers
- 8 olives, pitted
- 1 can (185 grams/6$^1/_2$ ounces) tuna, drained
- 110 grams/4 ounces/1 cup grated mozzarella cheese
- 1 red chilli, finely chopped
- 1 onion, peeled and sliced into rings

Method

1. Dissolve the yeast in the water.
2. Put the flour, salt, sugar and oil into a bowl.
3. Mix in the yeast mixture and set aside for 10 minutes. Knead the dough until it is soft. Cover the dough with a damp cloth and set aside until it doubles in volume.
4. Punch down the dough and knead again. Divide into two portions. Roll each portion into a flat round. Transfer to a pizza tray.
5. Spread each pizza base with Tomato Sauce and add the toppings.
6. Bake in a 180°C/350°F preheated oven for 25 minutes until the cheese is bubbly and the base of the pizza is cooked.

*TOMATO SAUCE

Ingredients

- 60 ml/2 fl oz/$^1/_4$ cup olive oil
- $^1/_2$ onion, peeled and finely chopped
- 3 cloves garlic, peeled and finely chopped
- 1 tablespoon chopped mixed fresh herbs: thyme, (Western) basil and oregano
- 1 can (411 grams/14$^1/_2$ ounces) Italian plum tomatoes, mashed
- salt
- sugar

Method

1. Heat the oil and sauté the onion, garlic and mixed herbs until fragrant.
2. Add the tomatoes, salt and sugar and simmer until the sauce thickens. Cool.

MINI PIZZA

Ingredients

- 30 grams/1 ounce dry yeast
- 1 teaspoon granulated sugar
- 250 ml/8 fl oz/1 cup lukewarm water
- 450 grams/1 pound/4 cups bread flour
- $^1/_4$ teaspoon salt
- 4 teaspoons olive oil
- Tomato Sauce*

Toppings

- 200 grams/7 ounces/1$^3/_4$ cups grated mozzarella cheese
- 10 beef frankfurters (hot dogs), chopped
- 1 onion, peeled and sliced
- 1 red capsicum (bell pepper), diced
- small bunch of parsley, chopped

Method

1. Dissolve the yeast and sugar in the water and set aside for 10 minutes.
2. Sift the flour and salt into a bowl.

3. Pour the yeast mixture and oil into the flour. Knead for about 10 minutes. Set aside the dough for about 1 hour in a warm area, until it doubles in volume.
4. Punch down the dough, knead for 5 minutes and leave it to rise for another 30 minutes.
5. Roll out the dough to the required size and place on a pizza tray.
6. Spread with Tomato Sauce and add the toppings.
7. Bake in a 180°C/350°F preheated oven for 20–25 minutes until the cheese is bubbly and the base of the pizza is cooked.

*TOMATO SAUCE

Ingredients

- 60 ml/2 fl oz/$^1/_4$ cup olive oil
- 1 large onion, peeled and diced
- 4 cloves garlic, peeled and finely chopped
- 1 teaspoon chopped fresh thyme
- 1 teaspoon chopped fresh oregano
- 1 can (411 grams/14$^1/_2$ ounces) Italian plum tomatoes, mashed
- 1 tablespoon tomato purée (tomato paste)
- salt
- freshly cracked black pepper
- 1 teaspoon sugar
- 1 tablespoon chopped parsley

Method

1. Heat the oil and sauté the onion, garlic, thyme and oregano until the onion is soft.
2. Add the tomatoes and tomato purée (tomato paste) and season with salt, pepper and sugar.
3. Add the parsley and simmer until the sauce thickens. Cool.

Note: You need not limit yourself to the above toppings. You can use seafood, chicken or minced (ground) beef with an assortment of vegetables and cheese.

Opposite: Tuna Pizza à la Mediterranean.

CHICKEN AND ASPARAGUS QUICHE

Ingredients

250 grams/9 ounces/1¹/₈ cup cold butter, diced

500 grams/1 pound, 1¹/₂ ounces/ 4³/₈ cups plain (all-purpose) flour

1 teaspoon lemon juice

water

Chicken Filling*

10 asparagus spears, cut into 2-cm/ 1-inch lengths

1 tomato, sliced into rounds

55 grams/2 ounces/¹/₂ cup grated cheddar cheese

Custard**

Method

1. Rub the butter into the flour and lemon juice until the mixture resembles breadcrumbs. Add water a little at a time to form a dough. Cover with plastic wrap and chill for 1 hour.

2. Roll out the dough and line a 23-cm /9-inch quiche pan. Line with aluminium foil and fill with beans.

3. Bake in a 180°C/350°F preheated oven for 20 minutes. Remove the aluminium foil and beans.

4. Put the Chicken Filling, asparagus and tomato into the quiche shell, sprinkle with cheese and pour in the Custard.

5. Bake in a 180°C/350°F preheated oven for 25 minutes.

Note: Chopped (Western) basil leaves may be sprinkled on top of the quiche before serving.

*CHICKEN FILLING

Ingredients

2 tablespoons cooking oil

1 onion, peeled and finely sliced

2 tablespoons tom yam paste

200 grams/7 ounces chicken breast, diced

Method

Heat the oil and sauté the onion until golden. Add the tom yam paste and chicken. Stir-fry for 2 minutes. Cool.

**CUSTARD

Ingredients

3 eggs

250 ml/8 fl oz/1 cup milk

125 ml/4 fl oz/¹/₂ cup whipping cream

salt

1 tablespoon chopped coriander leaves (cilantro)

Method

1. Whisk the eggs until light. Add the milk, cream and salt and continue whisking until fluffy. Strain.

2. Add the coriander leaves (cilantro).

SPICY PRAWN (SHRIMP) QUICHE

Ingredients

225 grams/8 ounces/1 cup cold butter, diced

500 grams/1 pound, 1¹/₂ ounces/ 4³/₈ cups plain (all-purpose) flour

2 tablespoons roasted sesame seeds

water

Prawn Filling*

1 tomato, sliced into rounds

Custard**

Method

1. Rub the butter into the flour until the mixture resembles breadcrumbs. Mix in the sesame seeds. Add water a little at a time to form a dough. Cover with plastic wrap and chill for 2 hours.

2. Roll out the dough and line a 23-cm /9-inch quiche pan. Prick the base with a fork. Line with aluminium foil and fill with beans.

3. Bake in a 180°C/350°F preheated oven for 20 minutes. Remove the aluminium foil and beans.

4. Put the Prawn Filling and tomato into the quiche shell and pour in the Custard.

5. Bake in a 180°C/350°F preheated oven for 25 minutes.

*PRAWN FILLING

Ingredients

2 tablespoons butter

¹/₂ onion, peeled and finely diced

1 tablespoon meat curry powder

300 grams/10¹/₂ ounces prawns (shrimps), shelled and deveined

1 sprig coriander leaves (cilantro), finely chopped

Method

Heat the butter and sauté the onion until soft. Add the meat curry powder, prawns (shrimps) and coriander leaves (cilantro). Cook until fragrant.

**CUSTARD

Ingredients

4 eggs

375 ml/12 fl oz/1¹/₂ cups whipping cream

salt

freshly cracked black pepper (optional)

Method

Beat the eggs with a fork. Add the cream and season with salt and pepper (optional). Strain.

Opposite: Chicken and Asparagus Quiche.

PHILLY BEEF SANDWICH

Ingredients

2 tablespoons butter
330 grams/11^1/$_2$ ounces beef loin, sliced
salt
freshly cracked black pepper
1 onion, peeled and finely sliced
1 green capsicum (bell pepper),
   finely sliced
60 ml/2 fl oz/^{1}/$_4$ cup Avocado
   Mayonnaise*
1 (30 cm/1 foot) French loaf,
   halved lengthways
lettuce leaves
2 tomatoes, finely sliced
100 grams/3^1/$_2$ ounces cheddar cheese,
   finely sliced

Method

1. Heat the butter and stir-fry the beef
   until it shrinks. Add salt and pepper.
   Remove the beef slices with a slotted
   spoon and set aside.

2. In the same pan, sauté the onion until
   soft. Add the capsicum (bell pepper)
   and stir-fry for 2 minutes.

3. Spread Avocado Mayonnaise on the
   inside of each bread half. Top with
   lettuce leaves, sautéed beef, onion
   and capsicum (bell pepper) mixture,
   tomatoes and cheese. Slice the bread
   into sandwich-sized pieces.

*AVOCADO MAYONNAISE

Ingredients

1 ripe avocado, stoned and peeled
250 ml/8 fl oz/1 cup mayonnaise
^{1}/$_2$ onion, peeled and finely chopped
1 red chilli, finely chopped
juice of ^{1}/$_2$ lime

1 clove garlic, peeled and finely ground
1 sprig coriander leaves (cilantro),
   finely chopped
salt
freshly cracked black pepper

Method

Using a fork or the back of a spoon, mash
the avocado. Add the remaining ingredients and refrigerate, covered, for 1 hour.

QUICK TUNA BURGERS

Ingredients

2 cans (185 grams/6^1/$_2$ ounces each)
   tuna, drained
2 tablespoons finely chopped onion
1 tablespoon finely chopped parsley
110 grams/4 ounces/1 cup breadcrumbs
1 tablespoon melted butter
^{1}/$_2$ teaspoon dry mustard
^{1}/$_2$ teaspoon salt
2 eggs, beaten
pinch of freshly ground black pepper
60 ml/2 fl oz/^{1}/$_4$ cup mayonnaise
butter for sautéing
6 burger buns, halved
1 head lettuce, torn into large pieces
4 tomatoes, sliced

Method

1. Combine the tuna, onion, parsley,
   breadcrumbs, melted butter, mustard,
   salt, eggs, pepper and mayonnaise.
   Shape into 4-cm/2-inch patties.

2. Sauté in butter until golden brown.

3. Fill the burger buns with tuna patties,
   lettuce and tomatoes.

AMERICAN CHICKEN POT PIE

Ingredients

55 grams/2 ounces/^{1}/$_4$ cup butter
1 large onion, peeled and diced
^{1}/$_4$ teaspoon dried thyme
^{1}/$_4$ teaspoon dried oregano
30 grams/1 ounce/^{1}/$_4$ cup plain
   (all-purpose) flour
10 button mushrooms, sliced
3 chicken breasts, diced
1 carrot, peeled and finely diced
2 celery stalks, finely diced
200 grams/7 ounces/1 cup green peas
2 potatoes, peeled and finely diced
750 ml/1^1/$_5$ pints/3 cups water
125 ml/4 fl oz/^{1}/$_2$ cup milk + milk
   for glazing
1 fresh bay leaf
pinch of ground nutmeg
salt
1 23-cm/9-inch quiche shell*,
   baked blind until fully cooked
1 portion quiche pastry dough*, chilled

Method

1. To make the filling, heat the butter and
   sauté the onion, thyme and oregano
   until fragrant. Stir in the flour and
   then the mushrooms.

2. Add the chicken, carrot, celery, green
   peas, potatoes, water and 125 ml/
   4 fl oz/^{1}/$_2$ cup milk. Add the bay leaf
   and nutmeg and season with salt.
   Simmer over low heat until thick.

3. Put the filling into the baked quiche
   shell. Roll the chilled pastry dough
   over it and brush the top with milk.

4. Bake in a 180°C/350°F preheated oven
   for 40 minutes until the top is golden.

* See the recipe for Chicken and Asparagus Quiche
on page 180.

Opposite: Philly Beef Sandwich.

PRAWN (SHRIMP) AND BROCCOLI TART

Ingredients

- 140 grams/5 ounces/⁵/₈ cup butter
- 140 grams/5 ounces/1¹/₄ cups grated cheddar cheese
- 225 grams/8 ounces/2 cups self-raising flour
- Prawn and Broccoli Filling*
- Cheese Custard**

Method

1. Combine the butter, cheese and flour. Press into a tart pan, as this pastry is too crumbly to roll out. Line with aluminium foil and fill with beans.
2. Bake in a 200°C/400°F preheated oven for 20 minutes until golden. Remove the aluminium foil and beans.
3. Put the Prawn and Broccoli Filling into the prepared tart shell and pour in the Cheese Custard.
4. Bake in a 200°C/400°F preheated oven for 20 minutes until the custard is golden brown.

*PRAWN AND BROCCOLI FILLING

Ingredients

- 3 tablespoons vegetable oil
- 170 grams/6 ounces broccoli florets, finely chopped
- 2 leeks, finely sliced
- 1 tablespoon chopped parsley
- 1 large carrot, peeled and grated
- 170 grams/6 ounces large prawns (shrimps), shelled, deveined and diced

Method

Heat the oil and sauté the broccoli, leeks, parsley, carrot and prawns (shrimps) until done.

**CHEESE CUSTARD

Ingredients

- 2 eggs, beaten
- 250 ml/8 fl oz/1 cup natural yoghurt
- 85 grams/3 ounces/³/₄ cup grated Gruyère cheese
- 3 tablespoons grated Parmesan cheese
- dash of double (heavy) cream
- salt
- freshly cracked black pepper

Method

Beat the eggs with the yoghurt, Gruyère cheese, Parmesan cheese and cream. Season with salt and pepper.

ACARAJE
(Spicy Bean Patties)

Ingredients

- 500 grams/1 pound, 1¹/₂ ounces black-eyed beans
- 2 onions, peeled and finely chopped
- 55 grams/2 ounces/¹/₂ cup dried prawns (shrimps), soaked in water, drained and pounded
- 6 bird's eye chillies, finely chopped
- 2 tablespoons chopped coriander leaves (cilantro)
- 1 egg, beaten
- salt
- freshly cracked black pepper
- cooking oil for deep-frying

Method

1. Soak the beans in water overnight. Wash them thoroughly, rubbing under running water to remove the skin.
2. Finely grind the beans and mix with all the remaining ingredients except oil.
3. Shape into balls (2 tablespoons each) and deep-fry until golden. Drain.

SPANOKOPITA
(Sesame Spinach Pie)

Ingredients

- 85 ml/2¹/₂ fl oz/¹/₃ cup olive oil
- 2 large onions, peeled and diced
- ¹/₂ teaspoon ground nutmeg
- 1 teaspoon powdered cumin
- 1 teaspoon chopped fresh dill
- 500 grams/1 pound, 1¹/₂ ounces spinach, blanched in salted water and drained
- juice of 1 lemon
- 1 tablespoon chopped parsley
- 2 eggs, beaten
- 45 grams/1¹/₂ ounces/¹/₄ cup feta cheese
- salt
- freshly cracked black pepper
- phyllo pastry
- 1 egg yolk, beaten
- 85 grams/3 ounces/¹/₂ cup sesame seeds

Method

1. Heat the oil and sauté the onions and nutmeg until fragrant and lightly browned.
2. Add the cumin, dill, spinach, lemon juice and parsley and cook for 2 minutes. Drain in a colander until cool.
3. Combine the spinach mixture with the eggs and cheese and season with salt and pepper. Wrap the mixture in phyllo pastry. Brush with beaten egg yolk and sprinkle with sesame seeds.
4. Bake in a 190°C/370°F preheated oven for 15 minutes.

Note: Cooked rice, raisins or pine nuts may be mixed into the filling. The unbaked pie can be frozen. Bake it just before serving. It is important to blanch the spinach in salted water, to retain its bright colour. Phyllo pastry, made with only flour and water, is also used in making apple strudel and baklava. Phyllo pastry dries quickly, so wrap or cover it with a damp towel.

Opposite: Acaraje (Spicy Bean Patties).

TAUHU GORENG SINGAPURA
(Singapore-Style Fried Bean Curd)

Ingredients

cooking oil for deep-frying
10 pieces hard bean curd
2 cucumbers, finely sliced
200 grams/7 ounces bean sprouts, tailed and blanched
Peanut Sauce*

Method

1. Heat the oil and deep-fry the bean curd until golden brown. Drain. Cut each into 8 pieces.

2. Arrange the bean curd in a serving dish and top with cucumber and bean sprouts.

3. Pour Peanut Sauce over and serve immediately.

*PEANUT SAUCE

Ingredients

15 cloves garlic, peeled
15 bird's eye chillies
600 grams/1 pound, 5 ounces/3^1/$_2$ cups peanuts, roasted
4–6 tablespoons grated palm sugar or brown sugar
5 tablespoons dark soy sauce
3 tablespoons vinegar or tamarind juice
250 ml/8 fl oz/1 cup water

Method

1. Grind the garlic, chillies and peanuts into a paste.

2. Add the palm sugar or brown sugar, soy sauce and vinegar or tamarind juice. Add the water and stir well.

3. Adjust the sweetness and sourness of the sauce according to taste.

THAI MONEY BAGS

Ingredients

60 ml/2 fl oz/^{1}/$_4$ cup cooking oil + cooking oil for deep-frying
4 cloves garlic, peeled and finely chopped
200 grams/7 ounces boneless chicken, finely diced
2 tablespoons oyster sauce
1 teaspoon light soy sauce
^{1}/$_2$ teaspoon ground white pepper
^{1}/$_2$ teaspoon sesame oil
6 Chinese mushrooms, soaked in hot water and finely sliced
6 water chestnuts, peeled and finely diced
200 grams/7 ounces small prawns (shrimps), shelled and deveined
55 grams/2 ounces/1^1/$_4$ cups glass noodles, soaked in hot water and drained
2 spring onions (scallions), finely chopped
1 teaspoon cornflour (cornstarch), mixed with 1 tablespoon water
20 pieces 10 cm x 10 cm/4 inch x 4 inch popia skin
10–12 dried spring onions (scallions)

Method

1. To make the filling, heat 60 ml/ 2 fl oz/^{1}/$_4$ cup cooking oil and add the garlic, chicken, oyster sauce, soy sauce, pepper and sesame oil. Sauté until the chicken is cooked. Add the mushrooms, water chestnuts and prawns (shrimps) and cook for 1 minute.

2. Add the glass noodles and spring onions (scallions). Mix well. Stir in the cornflour (cornstarch) mixture and cook until the sauce is thick. Cool.

3. Take 2 pieces of popia skin together and put 4 teaspoons of filling on top. Bring the ends of the popia skin to the centre and secure with a dried spring onion (scallion) to resemble a small pouch. Neaten the pouch top with scissors. Repeat until all the ingredients are used up.

4. Deep-fry the pouches until golden brown. Drain.

5. Serve hot with Thai chilli sauce.

OVOS RECHEADOS
(Stuffed Eggs)

Stuffed eggs are a popular first course in Portugal. They are also eaten as a snack. Accompanied by a salad and good bread, they make for a light lunch or supper.

Ingredients

4 large eggs, hard-boiled, shelled and halved
225 grams/8 ounces canned sardines in tomato sauce
approximately 1 tablespoon mayonnaise
1 teaspoon paprika
1 teaspoon lemon juice
salt
freshly cracked black pepper
1 tablespoon chopped parsley

Method

1. Scoop the egg yolks into a bowl and mash with the sardines. Work in enough mayonnaise to make a light paste. Add the paprika and lemon juice and season with salt and pepper.

2. Stuff the sardine mixture into the hollows left by the egg yolks and garnish with parsley.

Opposite: Thai Money Bags.

Alkaline water

Alkaline water (*kan sui* in Chinese) is available from Chinese grocery stores. Being corrosive, it is used to soften dried squid/cuttlefish before cooking.

Asam gelugur (*Garcinia atnoviridis*)

Asam gelugur is a tangerine-like fruit that is sliced thinly and dried in the sun. Light brown when fresh, it turns darker as it ages. Like tamarind, it is used to give acidity to cooked food.

Avocado (*Persea americana*)

Avocado, a pear-shaped fruit, is an import from Central America and grows easily in tropical Asia. The dark green to purple skin—although there is also a dark-skinned variety—covers an oily, soft, pale green flesh. Avocados can only be bought fresh and are always eaten raw. In the West they are used in salads and in hors d'oeuvres such as sauces, dips and mousses. In Asian cuisines, they are used in desserts.

To prepare an avocado for a recipe, halve it lengthways and separate the halves by gently twisting. Skew the knife slightly to prise out the seed. If the fruit is ripe, the skin may be peeled off easily. Cut avocado shortly before serving, as the flesh darkens when exposed to air.

Basil (*Ocimum* spp.)

Basil is a strong and pungent herb native to India. The Asian variety, also known as sweet basil, is milder than the Western one. Asian basil is an essential ingredient in the food of Thailand (where it is known as *horapa*, *mangklak*, *krapow*), Malaysia and Indonesia (*daun selasih*, *kemangi*). The leaves are usually added at the end of cooking to allow their sweet, fresh fragrance to balance the complex underlying spices. There is no real substitute for fresh Asian basil, since the dried leaves do not have the same flavour. However, fresh coriander leaves can be substituted in cooked dishes, while fresh mint leaves may be used as a substitute in salads.

The Western variety of basil, known as the 'prince of herbs' due to its superior flavour, is widely used in Mediterranean cuisines, especially Italian. The leaves are used fresh or dried: the fresh leaves have a clove-like taste, while the dried leaves taste like curry.

Bean curd

Bean curd or soy bean cake is made from ground soy beans. High in protein and low in calories, it comes in several forms: fresh, dried and pickled. Fresh bean curd has a delicate flavour not found in either the dried or the pickled form.

Hard bean curd comes in pieces about 6–8 cm (2$\frac{1}{2}$–3 inches) square. It is usually used for stuffing or is braised, stewed or deep-fried.

Soft bean curd is mainly steamed, scrambled or used in soups.

Dried bean curd sheets, which are sold in large pieces that need to be wiped with a damp cloth to clean and soften, are used as wrappers.

Bean sprouts

In Asia bean sprouts are grown from either mung beans (green beans) or soy beans, while in the West they are always grown from mung beans. If the sprouts are intended to be eaten raw they should be mung bean sprouts, as soy bean sprouts have to be cooked for 10 minutes before they can be eaten.

Bitter gourd (*Momordica charantia*)

Also known as bitter melon, bitter cucumber or balsam pear, bitter gourd is used in tropical south Chinese and Southeast Asian cuisines. Before cooking, the central pithy portion of this elongated vegetable is discarded and the rest is thinly sliced and sprinkled with salt to draw out the liquid and some of the bitterness.

Candlenut

The hard, oily candlenut comes from the candleberry tree (*Aleurites moluccana*), which is native to eastern Asia and some Pacific islands. Known as *kemiri* in Indonesia and *buah keras* in Malaysia and Singapore, the nut is usually ground and used as a thickening and flavouring agent.

Macadamia nuts or Brazil nuts may be used as substitutes. However, both are sweeter than the slightly bitter candlenut.

Capers

Capers are the unopened buds of the caper bush (*Capparis spinosa*), native to the Mediterranean region. They are always used pickled—as a condiment, in salads and sauces (particularly with fish), as a garnish for appetisers and as a pizza topping.

Capsicum (*Capsicum annuum*)

Native to tropical America and the West Indies, capsicums are usually classed as being either sweet or hot and come in many colours and sizes. Sweet capsicums (bell peppers) are mild in taste and can be eaten raw or cooked. Chilli capsicums (pimientos) are used almost exclusively as a seasoning. The most familiar capsicums are the sweet, green ones that change to red as they ripen. They are used in salads, stews and sauces and can also be stuffed. The small red or green conical capsicums are the fiery chillies that feature in Indian curries as well as Mexican and Latin American dishes. Capsicums are available fresh all year round, but they are also sold canned.

Cardamom (*Elettaria cardamomum*)

Cardamom is the world's most expensive spice after saffron. Cardamom pods are the dried fruits of a perennial plant of the ginger family indigenous to Sri Lanka and south India. The pale green oval pods, which are the best variety, contain 15–20 brown or black seeds. The white pods are simply green pods that have been bleached in the sun.

Celery (*Apium graveolens var. dulce*)

Asian celery (sometimes called Chinese celery) is much smaller, darker green and stronger in flavour than the thick, pale green Western variety. The leaves and stalks of Asian celery are used to flavour soups, while Western celery can be sliced and stir-fried with seafood or poultry and cooked in stews.

Chilli (*Capsicum frutescens*)

Native to Mexico, chillies are now available in many forms: fresh, dried, powdered, flaked, as well as in the form of sauces, sambals and paste. They range from mild to wild, and the smaller the chilli the hotter it is, e.g., bird's eye chilli. Chillies are used either unripe, when they are green, or ripe, after they turn red. Ripe chillies are hotter than green ones. Red chillies are usually pounded or ground into a paste, chopped or used whole for flavouring, or cut in different ways for garnishing. Green chillies are generally used whole for flavouring or cut into various shapes for garnishing. Both red and green chillies are also available pickled. Dried chillies are pounded or ground and used for flavouring and seasoning.

Cinnamon (*Cinnamomum zeylanicum*)

Cinnamon, the edible bark of a tree native to Sri Lanka, is probably the most popular cooking spice in the Western world. The innermost layer of the bark is sold as thin, fragile quills in India (*darchini*), Sri Lanka (*kurundu*), Indonesia (*kayu manis*) and Malaysia and Singapore (*kulit kayu manis*) and is used for flavouring meat, poultry and desserts. The spice is also available powdered, but its flavour and aroma dissipate rather quickly in this form.

Clove (*Eugenia aromatica*)

Cloves are actually the flower buds of a tree of the myrtle family indigenous to the Maluku Islands (Moluccas) or the Spice Islands. The buds are harvested and dried under the sun for days. Cloves have a stronger flavour than most other spices and are therefore used in smaller quantities.

Coconut (*Cocos nucifera*)

Coconut is indispensable in Malaysian, Singaporean, Indonesian and Thai kitchens. Coconut milk is not the water found in the middle of the coconut; rather, it is the liquid extracted from soaking fresh grated coconut in water and then straining it. There are two types of coconut milk: thick milk comes from the first squeeze of grated coconut with a small amount of water, while thin milk is obtained from the second squeeze with considerably more water.

Roasted grated coconut is often added to enrich certain dishes. This is obtained by roasting fresh grated coconut, stirring constantly, in a dry pan over low heat until it turns golden brown. If desiccated coconut is used, the flesh should be moistened with a little water before roasting. However, desiccated coconut lacks the rich flavour of fresh coconut.

Kerisik is obtained by grating the flesh of a mature coconut, roasting it until golden brown and then pounding or grinding it until the oil seeps out. If fresh coconut is not available, desiccated coconut can be used instead. Called *poyah* or *ambu-ambu* in Indonesia, *kerisik* is used a lot in Malaysian and Indonesian dishes.

Coriander leaves (*Coriandrum sativum*)

Also known as cilantro or Chinese parsley, coriander is indigenous to southern Europe. All parts of the plant can be used, even the roots, which are an essential ingredient in Thai cooking. Coriander leaves are used to flavour and garnish dishes.

1. *Salam* leaves **2.** Lemon grass **3.** Ferntops **4.** Torch ginger bud **5.** Basil (*selasih*) leaves
6. Pea eggplants **7.** Kaffir limes **8.** *Kesum* leaves **9.** Turmeric leaf **10.** Galangal **11.** Curry leaves
12. Young jackfruit **13.** Pandan leaves **14.** Kaffir lime leaves **15.** Turmeric

Coriander seeds

With their clean, lemony flavour, coriander seeds are a major component of most curry powders used in India, Sri Lanka, Indonesia, Malaysia and other countries. Freshly ground coriander is more fragrant than coriander that is purchased already powdered.

Couscous

Couscous, a grain-like cereal, is a staple of Moroccan cuisine. It is made from semolina, which is coarsely ground durum wheat. The semolina grains are sprinkled with flour and water, then rubbed either by hand or by machine into tiny pellets. Couscous may be steamed and served like pasta, or it can be served as an accompaniment to other main dishes. It can also be mixed with honey, fruit and nuts and served as a dessert.

Crisp-fried shallots

Crisp-fried shallots are shallots that have been sliced fine and deep-fried in hot oil until golden brown. They are used for flavouring and garnishing. To make them at home, peel the shallots and finely slice them crosswise. Deep-fry in hot oil over low heat, stirring briskly all the while. Turn off the heat as soon as they turn a pale brown. Remove and drain on absorbent paper until cool. Store in an airtight container.

Cucumber (*Cucumis sativus*)

Ancient cultivated vegetables believed to be indigenous to India, cucumbers come in many varieties, shapes and sizes. Available all year round, they are usually eaten raw in salads. They can also be bought pickled.

Curry leaves (*Murraya koenigii*)

Sprigs of small, shiny, pointed leaves with a distinctive fragrance, curry leaves are used most frequently in south India (*meetha neem, karipattar, karuvepillay*), Sri Lanka (*karapincha*), Malaysia and Singapore (*daun kari*) and Fiji. Fresh curry leaves are normally sautéed with onions while making curry. Dried curry leaves, which are probably easier to find in Western countries, are not as strongly flavoured, but they serve the purpose.

Dill (*Anethum graveolens*)

Dill, a herb that comes from the parsley family, is indigenous to southern Europe and western Asia. Sometimes called dill weed, it is best known for its affinity with fish. It is also used fresh or dried in soups, egg dishes and sauces.

Dried prawns (shrimps)

Dried prawns are boiled or steamed prawns that have been shelled and dried. The best dried prawns are a deep salmon pink. They should not be hard or smell strongly of ammonia. Dried prawns are used—either whole or pounded—in several Asian cuisines, both as a flavouring agent and as the main ingredient.

Dried radish

Dried radish is known in Chinese as *chai poh*. It is obtained by cleaning and peeling white radish, cutting it into even-sized pieces and preserving it with spices and salt. The crisp golden brown pieces that result are delicious eaten as a relish.

Eggplant/brinjal

Originating in Asia, the eggplant (also known as aubergine in Europe) comes in a number of shapes, sizes and colours, with a surprising variation in flavour. Garden eggplants (*Solanum melongena*) vary considerably in shape, size and colour—from smallish spheres of white, pale green, white streaked with purple, mauve and shades of yellow to rich, deep purple specimens that weigh around 1 kilogram/ 2 pounds, 3 ounces. Eggplant is popular in China, Japan, India, Indonesia, Malaysia, the Philippines, Sri Lanka and Thailand.

Pea eggplants (*Solanum torvum*) grow in clusters of tiny spheres with a tough skin and bitter taste. They are used whole in curries in Malaysia (*terung pipit*), Indonesia (*tekokak*) and Thailand (*makhua puang*) and eaten raw with *nam prik* (sauce or dip) in Thailand.

Fennel (*Foeniculum vulgare*)

Fennel is used as both a vegetable and a herb in Europe. But in Asia only the seeds are used. The seeds are similar to cumin but slightly whiter and fatter. They have a sweet fragrance and flavour and are used in far smaller amounts than are cumin and coriander.

Fenugreek (*Trigonella foenum-graecum*)

The seeds and tender sprouted leaves of fenugreek, native to Europe and Asia, are both edible. The seeds, with their bitter flavour, are an important component of Indian curry powders. The seeds are also used whole in some Sri Lankan and Malaysian dishes, particularly seafood curries.

Ferntops (*Athyrium esculentum*)

The Malaysian and Indonesian varieties of jade green, immature curling heads of edible ferns are called *pucuk paku* or *daun pakis*. The tips are cooked as a vegetable, like fiddleheads or bracken fern, which make good substitutes. Sometimes the tips are blanched and put in salads.

Four-angled bean (*Psophocarpus tetragonolobus*)

Other names for the four-angled bean are asparagus bean, asparagus pea, winged bean, frilly bean, manilla bean, Goa bean, Mauritius bean and princess pea. The pods of the bean are very decorative, with four serrated edges and tiny seeds contained inside a central 'rib'. They are generally green, but they may also be pink, purple or red. In Asian cooking, four-angled beans are usually stir-fried or put in salads.

Galangal

Greater galangal (*Alpinia galanga*), called *lengkuas* (Malaysia), *laos* (Indonesia) or *kha* (Thailand), is native to Malaysia and Java. It has a delicate flavour and is normally used fresh in Malaysian, Indonesian and Thai cooking. When the fresh variety is not available, dried or powdered galangal can be used instead. In a recipe, 1 tablespoon chopped fresh galangal is equivalent to 1 teaspoon powdered galangal.

Lesser galangal or aromatic ginger (*Kaempferia galanga*), called *cekur* (Malaysia and Singapore) or *kencur* (Indonesia), is a smaller variety of galangal. It has a strong flavour, and therefore only a small quantity needs to be used. In a recipe, 1 teaspoon chopped lesser galangal is equivalent to $1/2$ teaspoon powdered lesser galangal.

Gherkin

Gherkins are small cucumbers grown exclusively for pickling. They usually accompany meat patés, cold meats and grilled meats. Gherkins can also be used in salads and dressings.

Ginger (*Zingiber officinale*)

Ginger, a fleshy rhizome, is used in the West to make gingerbread, ginger beer, candied ginger and chocolate ginger. Fresh ginger is a basic ingredient in many Asian cuisines. It is usually sliced, finely chopped, pounded or ground and used in savoury dishes. Sometimes the juice is extracted and used.

Hot bean paste

Hot bean paste, used in Szechuan cooking, is a mixture of fermented soy beans, ground hot chilli and seasoning. It is available ready-made.

Jackfruit (*Artocarpus heterophyllus*)

The jackfruit tree, native to India's Western Ghats, bears the world's largest fruit. The fruit is eaten both young and ripe.

Green, with thick, sharp spines, the starchy young jackfruit is usually cooked as a vegetable. It is a staple source of starch in many Asian and South Pacific countries, where it is fried, roasted or boiled.

Kaduk leaf (*Piper sarmentosum*)

Native to Borneo and Indonesia, the *kaduk* leaf or pointed pepper is now widely cultivated in Southeast Asia and China. It is a tall-branched herb with a hairy stem.

The thin, oval *kaduk* leaves smell and taste slightly pungent. In Malaysia they are usually eaten as a vegetable— either raw as an *ulam* or blanched in boiling water as an appetiser.

Kaffir lime (*Citrus hystrix, C. papedia*)

The kaffir lime is a round, dark green citrus fruit with a distinct nipple on the stem end and a thick, bumpy, wrinkled rind. The rind, which has a sharp, bitter-sweet taste, is used in Thailand (*makrut, som makrut*), Malaysia and Singapore (*limau purut*), Indonesia (*jeruk purut*) and other countries in Southeast Asia to impart a delicate lemony flavour to dishes.

Kaffir lime leaves may be recognised by their two distinct sections. The fresh or dried leaves are most commonly used whole in soups or curries. If kaffir lime leaves are not available, the tender new leaves of lime, lemon or grapefruit may be used as a substitute.

Kalamansi (Musk lime) (*Citrus microcarpa, C. mitis*)

A small variety of lime, the *kalamansi* or musk lime is 2–3 cm (1–1$1/2$ inches) in diameter. Green or greenish yellow in colour, it is more fragrant than the lime. *Kalamansi* are generally used to flavour Southeast Asian curries, sambals and noodle soups. If they are not available, they may be substituted with half-ripe kumquats or even lemons.

1. (Western) Basil leaves **2.** Oregano **3.** Tarragon **4.** Dill **5.** Sage **6.** Thyme **7.** Rosemary

Kesum leaves/polygonum leaves/Vietnamese mint (*Persicaria odorata*, syn. *Polygonum adoratum*)

The narrow, pointed polygonum leaves are not a variety of mint. The leaves are an essential ingredient in the famous Singaporean/Malaysian seafood noodle soup, laksa, and are therefore known in Malaysia and Singapore as *daun laksa* (laksa leaf). They are also known as *daun kesum*. In Vietnam, where they are called *rau ram*, they are used in salads or eaten fresh with the popular cha gio.

Lemon (*Citrus limon*)

Native to India, the lemon is the most versatile of all citrus fruit. It takes just a few drops of lemon juice to enhance the flavour of delicate fish or poultry dishes, creams and pies. The acid in the juice also prevents cut fruit from turning brown when exposed to air.

Lemon grass (*Cymbopogon citratus*)

Lemon grass, a long lemon-scented grass, is popular for flavouring curries and soups in Malaysia and Singapore (*serai*), Indonesia (*sere*), Thailand (*takrai*) and other Southeast Asian countries. Only the pale lower portion of the stem, with the tough outer layers peeled away, is used for cooking. If lemon grass is not available, two or three strips of thinly peeled lemon zest can be used as a substitute.

Lime (*Citrus aurantifolia*)

The lime is a round, dark green, thin-skinned citrus fruit that originated in India. With its strong, sour juice, it is closely related to the lemon and is often used as a substitute for the latter. It is used in juices, cocktails, pickles and curries.

Mango (*Mangifera indica*)

Mangoes are native to India and Malaysia, but they are now grown in many countries. At their best, mangoes have bright orange flesh and a strong, sweet fragrance. They vary in size and shape, from little round or oblong ones to heavy ones almost the size of melons. Some are long, slender and green skinned even when fully ripe.

Ripe mangoes are combined with other ingredients to make delicious sweets or cooling drinks. Semi-ripe mangoes are invaluable for making mango chutney, because they hold their shape during cooking. Green, unripe mangoes can be pickled, while mature but under-ripe mangoes are used in salads.

Mozzarella cheese

A soft cheese with a rather moist texture, mozzarella cheese has a mild, creamy taste and is used widely in cooking, for instance in pizza and pasta. It is an Italian unripened curd cheese that was originally made from buffalo's milk but is now obtained exclusively from cow's milk. This cheese is available in rounds and slabs as well as already grated.

Mushrooms

Mushrooms, used extensively in Chinese cooking, come in many varieties. Dried Chinese mushrooms—either black or very dark brown with white markings—have a distinctive flavour. Button mushrooms are available both canned and fresh.

Shiitake (*Lentinus edodes*) are also referred to as fragrant mushrooms, golden oak mushrooms and Chinese black mushrooms. These earthy-smelling fungi have gold to deep brown caps with a slight bloom and creamy gills. They are available both fresh and dried.

Nam pla (Fish sauce)

Fish sauce is a thin, salty, brown liquid obtained by packing fish with salt in wooden barrels and leaving it to ferment for a few months. This pungent seasoning is called *nam pla* in Thailand and *nuoc nam* in Vietnam.

Noodles

Fresh yellow noodles are made from flour and eggs and are used mainly in Hokkien dishes. However, Malay and Indian cooks use them for mee rebus and mee goreng. Spaghetti is a good substitute if fresh yellow noodles are not available.

Known as kway teow or sa hor fun, fresh rice flour noodles are flat and wide. They are made from rice flour and have a creamy texture and mild flavour.

Fresh laksa noodles, also made from rice flour, are as thick as spaghetti. Dried rice vermicelli can be used as a substitute if fresh laksa noodles are not available.

The vermicelli-like glass noodles are made from mung bean flour. They are also called cellophane noodles or bean starch noodles. They should be soaked in water before being added to boiling soups or stir-fried vegetables. Glass noodles are used in Japanese, Thai, Burmese, Vietnamese, Chinese, Malaysian, Philippine and Indonesian cooking.

Olives (*Olea europea*)

Olives are the fruit of a tree native to the Mediterranean coastal region. There are several varieties of olives, including black olives and green olives. The latter are often stuffed with red peppers or pimiento. Fresh olives have an intensely bitter flesh, and the fruit are therefore generally eaten pickled.

Oregano (*Origanum vulgare*)

Also known as wild marjoram, the aromatic oregano is native to Asia, Europe and north Africa. The leaves of the herb, usually used in their dried form, are best known for their use in Italian dishes, especially pizza. The Greek varieties are collectively called *rigani*, and their flowers are used to garnish meat dishes.

Palm sugar

Palm sugar is made from the sap of the palm tree. Fresh palm sap is boiled down shortly after collection to make a concentrated heavy palm syrup. This syrup is poured into bamboo sections to form cylindrical shapes, or into small shallow bowls to form shallow hemispheres. The sugar ranges from almost white to pale honey-gold to a deep, dark brown, with varying consistency. Palm sugar is used in Malaysia (*gula melaka, gula kabung*) Indonesia (*gula jawa, aren*) and Thailand (*nam taan pep, nam taan bik, nam taan mapraow*)—for both savoury and sweet dishes.

Pandan leaf (*Pandanus amaryllifolius*)

The long, narrow pandan leaves are also known as pandanus leaves. They are used in both savoury and sweet dishes in Malaysia, Singapore, Indonesia (*daun pandan*) and Thailand (*bai toey*). These leaves, with their delicate flavour, are as essential to Asian cooking as vanilla is to Western. Pieces of marinated chicken are wrapped in pandan leaves and deep-fried so that the flavour of the leaves is imparted to the chicken. The leaves are also pounded and strained to lend flavour and colour to sweets.

Papaya (*Carica papaya*)

Indigenous to Central America, papayas range in size from very small to very large, and they are eaten both green and ripe. When ripe, the papaya has soft, juicy flesh and a fairly sweet taste (similar to apricot) and makes a good dessert or breakfast fruit. The unripe fruit, which has crisp, firm flesh, can be cooked as a vegetable and is also used to make preserves and pickles.

The fruit is very popular in Asia, where the flowers, leaves and young stems of the papaya tree are also cooked and eaten.

Parmesan cheese

The granular Parmesan is one of Italy's best-known cheeses. Made from cow's milk, this cheese is made in wheel shapes. When fully mature (golden in colour), it is grated and used in cooking.

Pepper (*Piper nigrum*)

Peppers are small, round berries that grow in trailing clusters. They start off a deep green and turn red as they ripen.

Black pepper is obtained by drying the green berries in the sun, which makes the outer skin black and shrivelled.

White pepper is obtained by packing the ripe berries in sacks, soaking them in slow-flowing water for eight days and then rubbing off the softened outer skin. The inner portion is then dried in the sun for several days until it turns a creamy white. White pepper is hotter than black pepper, but it is not as fragrant.

---

1. Gherkins **2.** Capers **3.** Grated cheese **4.** Saffron strands **5.** *Kerisik* **6.** Roasted grated coconut **7.** Wheat couscous **8.** Dried prawns (shrimps) **9.** Dried squid **10.** Parmesan cheese **11.** Star anise **12.** Cinnamon sticks **13.** Cloves **14.** Cardamoms **15.** *Asam gelugur* **16.** Candlenuts **17.** Tamarind pulp **18.** Black olives **19.** Stuffed green olives **20.** Palm sugar **21.** Preserved radish **22.** Glass noodles

Pineapple
(*Ananas comosus*)

Native to South America, the pineapple is really a cluster of fruits of the Ananas tree that combine to form one 'multiple fruit'. The pineapple is one of the most popular of all tropical fruit. Available all year round, it makes an excellent dessert fruit. It can be bought fresh or canned. The fruit is delicious eaten ripe. In Asia semi-ripe pineapple is used in sour soups and curries.

Pumpkin
(*Cucurbita moschata*)

Originating in tropical South or Central America, pumpkins are now widely distributed throughout the tropics. The vegetables—which can weigh up to 4–5 kilograms/8³/₄ pounds–10 pounds, 15 ounces—come in various shapes and sizes. The colour of the flesh ranges from yellow to orange. Pumpkins are eaten both as a fruit and as a vegetable. They are puréed to make soups, roasted, fried or baked. They can also be stuffed and cooked.

Rosemary
(*Rosmarinus officinalis*)

Rosemary, an aromatic herb native to the Mediterranean region, grows wild over most of Europe and North America. Its hard, spiky leaves contain oil of camphor and are widely used for flavouring meat dishes, chicken and fish.

Saffron

Saffron strands are the dried stigmas of the autumn-flowering crocus (*Crocus sativus*) native to Asia Minor. The flowers have to be picked by hand, and about 70,000 flowers (each has three hair-like stigmas) are needed to obtain a kilogram of saffron strands. When dried, the stigmas lose about 80 percent of their weight. Therefore, saffron is clearly the most expensive spice in the world. It is intensely aromatic, with a slightly pungent flavour, and imparts a beautiful yellow colour to dishes. It is available in powdered form, but that is considered inferior in flavour to the strands.

Sage
(*Salvia officinalis*)

Sage, a herb native to the northern Mediterranean coast, has downy leaves and a strong flavour. It comes in a variety of colours and flavours. Green sage is used in stuffing, particularly for pork and duck, as well as in stews and casseroles.

Salam leaf
(*Eugenia polyantha*)

The tough, aromatic *salam* leaf, similar in shape and size to the bay leaf, contains volatile oils. The fresh leaves (*daun salam*) are used whole in Indonesian curries to impart a unique flavour. If *salam* leaves are not available they may be substituted with curry leaves, which are somewhat similar in flavour.

Soy sauce

Soy sauce, used to flavour and colour food, is made from salted soy beans. There are three types of soy sauce.

Light soy sauce is the type most commonly used for flavouring.

Dark soy sauce is a black, thicker sauce with a stronger flavour. It is generally used in stews for its flavour and colour.

Sweet soy sauce is a thick, sweet sauce used in dishes of Javanese origin.

Spring onion
(*Allium fistulosum*)

Spring onions, known as scallions in the United States, have long, thin leaves, with sometimes a white bulb at the base. Both the white and the green portions are chopped and used for garnishing.

Star anise
(*Illicium verum*)

Star anise comes from a tree belonging to the magnolia family. The dried eight-pointed star-shaped seed pod is used for flavouring meat and poultry dishes in Malaysia, Singapore, Indonesia (*bunga lawang*), China (*baht gok*) and Vietnam (*hoi*).

Tamarind pulp

Tamarind pulp is obtained from the ripe pods of a plant (*tamarindus indica*) of the *Leguminosae* family. The rich brown pulp, which surrounds large, shiny brown seeds, is separated from the reddish brown shell by a few strong fibres running the length of the pod between the pulp and the shell.

Tamarind pulp is soaked in water, squeezed and kneaded to disperse it in the water and then strained before being used to give a fragrant sourness to food. Called *asam jawa* in Malaysia, it is used in most Malaysian dishes.

Tarragon (*Artemesia dracunculus*)

Commonly used in French cooking, tarragon is native to southern Europe. The aromatic herb is used in sauces, soups, fish dishes and salads. Russian tarragon is inferior in flavour and has a coarser leaf. Tarragon is available fresh, dried or powdered.

Tempe

Tempe, made from fermented soy beans, is used a lot in Malaysian and Indonesian cooking. The beans are soaked overnight, hulled, steamed for 30 minutes, soaked overnight again, inoculated with a pure culture of *Rhizopus oligosporu*, wrapped in large leaves and set aside for 24 hours.

Thyme
(*Thymus vulgaris*)

Thyme is native to southern Europe and along the Mediterranean coast. This perennial is one of the most popular and best-known herbs. It has a strong, sharp taste and is used to flavour soups, stews, roast meat and poultry stuffing.

Tomato (*Lycopersicum esculentum*)

Native to South America, tomatoes are used extensively in India and Southeast Asia. They come in many shapes and sizes. Red and green tomatoes can be bought fresh and eaten either raw or cooked. Red tomatoes are eaten raw in salads and relishes and added to curries. They are also available dried or in the forms of juice, purée and ketchup. Green tomatoes are used in pickles and chutneys.

Torch ginger bud/flower
(*Nicolaia elatior*)

Torch ginger bud/flower, which has a delicate aroma, is the bud/flower of a tall and aromatic ginger native to Southeast Asia. In Indonesia, where it is called *kecombrong*, it is cooked with fish to reduce the smell or sliced as part of a vegetable salad. In Malaysia it is known as *bunga kantan* or *bunga siantan*. In Thailand the flowers (*kaalaa*) are served raw with *nam prik*.

Turmeric
(*Curcuma domestica*)

Turmeric, a knobbly rhizome, looks like ginger except it is bright orange in colour. It is used fresh in Southeast Asian cooking to colour and flavour food. It can also be bought dried or powdered. In a recipe, 1 tablespoon chopped fresh turmeric is equivalent to ¹/₄ teaspoon powdered turmeric.

The large turmeric leaf is used in Malaysia, Singapore and Indonesia (*daun kunyit*) for flavouring food.

Zucchini
(*Cucurbita pepo*)

Zucchini, a small variety of marrow, does not need peeling. It can simply be topped, tailed, sliced and eaten raw with dips. It can also be steamed, or battered and fried.

---

1. Papaya **2.** Pineapple **3.** Capsicum (Bell pepper) **4.** Lemon **5.** Eggplant **6.** Avocado **7.** *Kalamansi* **8.** Zucchini **9.** Four-angled bean **10.** Cucumber **11.** Ripe mango **12.** Tomato **13.** Unripe mango **14.** Pumpkin

INDEX